1973

University of St. Francis
GEN 811.5 P876ch
Henault

S0-BNK-925

The Merrill Studies
in
The Cantos

CHARLES E. MERRILL STUDIES

Under the General Editorship of
Matthew J. Bruccoli and Joseph Katz

LIBRARY
College of St. Francis
JOLIET, ILL.

The Merrill Studies
in
The Cantos

Compiled by

Marie Hénault
St. Michael's College

Charles E. Merrill Publishing Company
A Bell & Howell Company
Columbus, Ohio

The author and publisher gratefully acknowledge the following for permission to quote from the works of Ezra Pound: *Letters of Ezra Pound 1907-1941,* edited by D. D. Paige. Copyright 1950 by Ezra Pound. *The Cantos of Ezra Pound.* Copyright 1934, 1937, 1940, 1948, 1956, 1959, 1968 by Ezra Pound. Ezra Pound, *Personae.* Copyright 1926 by Ezra Pound. Reprinted by permission of New Directions Publishing Corporation.

Copyright © 1971 by Charles E. Merrill Publishing Company, Columbus, Ohio. All rights reserved. No part of this book may be reproduced in any form, electronic or mechanical, including photocopy, recording, or any information storage and retrieval system without permission in writing from the publisher.

ISBN: 0-675-09182-9

Library of Congress Catalog Card Number: 78-168862

1 2 3 4 5 6 7 8 — 78 77 76 75 74 73 72 71

Printed in the United States of America

811.5
P876ch

Preface

The Cantos of Ezra Pound, unquestionably the longest poem of the age, makes other long poems such as *Four Quartets, the Bridge,* and *Paterson* seem short. In addition to the magnificence of its more than 800-page length, *The Cantos* also has a magnificence of conception and execution plus a continuing and absorbing interest to which the eight published books and innumerable articles devoted solely to the poem testify.

The one agreement among these many scholars and critics seems to be about the poem's importance. To reflect this I have eschewed collecting essays on each of the eight main division of *The Cantos,* in favor of presenting unusually valuable pieces. Most of these view the whole poem, deal with its major themes and preoccupations, or, while concentrating on individual sections, look to the whole poem as well.

These articles make clear, I think, what the poem is—a sequence, an extraordinarily long one with its parts linked together by the themes and subjects of the Odyssean voyage: metamorphosis, continuity, flux, light, love, the good leader, the good society. Begun "about 1904" according to Pound, *The Cantos* has been appearing at irregular intervals for over sixty years, from the World War I period up to the present. Its main parts now are the following:

TITLE	CANTOS	NO. OF PAGES
1) *A Draft of XXX Cantos* (1930)	1–30	149
2) *Eleven New Cantos: XXXI–XLI* (1934)	31–41	56
3) *The Fifth Decad of Cantos* (1937)	42–51	46
4) *Cantos LII–LXXI* (1940)	52–71	167

66331

Within these eight published parts Cantos are grouped according to theme and subject matter: the Renaissance Cantos, for example, 8–19, with Malatesta as a principal figure, 13 a paradise, and 14–16 a hell; the American history Cantos, 30–41, Jefferson; the Chinese history Cantos, 53–61, Confucius; the John Adams Cantos, 62–71; and other groups. *The Pisan Cantos*, part five above, is a Purgatorio and *Thrones*, part seven, a Paradiso. But, as Pound himself has said, *The Cantos* does not adhere to the tripartite scheme of Dante's *Divine Comedy* in any regular manner.

The most recent section, part eight, would be more exactly designated "Drafts, Notes, and Fragments—Cantos 100 and 110–117," for it contains two fragments of Canto 100; drafts of Cantos 110, 113, 114, and 116; notes for Cantos 111 and 117; and fragments of Cantos 112 and 115. This 1969 addition to *The Cantos* compellingly suggests the difficulty of concluding a work as seemingly interminable as the poem is. For instance it now seems that, unlike Joyce's *Work in Progress* which became *Finnegans Wake*, *this* work in progress will never be called anything other than—*The Cantos*. Thus rather than a revealing title, a thunderous conclusion, a Canto or a group of Cantos that interweaves all themes, it seems likely that the poem will sometime—soon, no doubt, considering Pound's great age—simply cease appearing, and so take a place among the world's unfinished works.

The essays collected here have been chosen so as to avoid including many good essays already available in one or the other of the anthologies on Pound's poetry, several of which are still in print. At the same time, however, I did not exclude for this reason essays of extraordinary importance such as those by Hugh Kenner and Forrest Read, which appeared respectively in Noel Stock's *Ezra Pound—Perspectives: Essays in Honor of His Eightieth Birthday* (1965) and Eva Hesse's *New Approaches to Ezra Pound* (1969). Yet *Studies in The Cantos* is, I believe, generally unrepetitive. The first section contains the poet's brief statements about *The Cantos* in letters and in an interview. In the second section essays about the method of *The Cantos* come first, others on specific Cantos follow, and those about theme and the whole poem finish the book.

M.H.

Contents

1. Statements by Ezra Pound

From a letter to Sarah Perkins Cope, January 15, 1934

Skip anything you don't understand and go on till you pick it up again. All tosh about *foreign* languages making it difficult. The quotes are all either explained at once by repeat or they are definitely *of* the things indicated. If reader don't know what an elefant is, then the word is obscure.

I admit there are a couple of Greek quotes, one along in 39 that can't be understood without Greek, but *if* I can drive the reader to learning at least that much Greek, she or he will indubitably be filled with a durable gratitude. And if not, what harm? I can't conceal the fact that the Greek language existed.

From *Selected Letters, 1907–1941*, D. D. Paige, ed. (New York: New Directions, 1950), pp. 250–51. Copyright 1950 by Ezra Pound. Reprinted by permission of New Directions Publishing Corporation.

From a letter to Hubert Creekmore, February, 1939

I believe that when finished, *all* foreign words in *The Cantos*, Gk., etc., will be underlinings, not necessary to the sense, in one way. I mean a complete sense will exist without them; it will be there in the American text, but the Greek, ideograms, etc., will indicate a *duration* from whence or since when. If you find any *briefer* means of getting this repeat or resonance, tell papa, and I will try to employ it.

From *Selected Letters, 1907–1941*, D. D. Paige, ed. (New York: New Directions, 1950), pp. 322–23. Copyright 1950 by Ezra Pound. Reprinted by permission of New Directions Publishing Corporation.

... All typographic disposition, placings of words *on* the page, is intended to facilitate the reader's intonation, whether he be reading silently to self or aloud to friends. Given time and technique I might even put down the musical notation of passages or "breaks into song."

There is *no intentional* obscurity. There is condensation to maximum attainable. It is impossible to make the deep as quickly comprehensible as the shallow.

The order of words and sounds *ought* to induce the proper reading; proper tone of voice, etc., but can *not* redeem fools for idiocy, etc. If the goddam violin string is not tense, no amount of bowing will help the player. And *so* forth.

As to the *form* of *The Cantos*: All I can say or pray is: wait till it's there. I mean wait till I get 'em written and then if it don't show, I will start exegesis. I haven't an Aquinas-map; Aquinas *not* valid now.

Ezra Pound

From an interview with Donald Hall, 1962

I began *The Cantos* about 1904, I suppose. I had various schemes, starting in 1904 or 1905. The problem was to get a form — something elastic enough to take the necessary material. It had to be a form that wouldn't exclude something merely because it didn't fit. In the first sketches, a draft of the present first *Canto* was the third.

Obviously you haven't got a nice little road map such as the middle ages possessed of Heaven. Only a musical form would take the material, and the Confucian universe as I see it is a universe of interacting strains and tensions.

From [George Plimpton, ed.], *Writers at Work: The Paris Review Interviews*, Second Series (New York: The Viking Press, 1965), pp. 38, 39, 56, 57, 58. Copyright © 1963 by The Paris Review, Inc. All Rights Reserved. Reprinted by permission of The Viking Press, Inc. and Martin Secker & Warburg Ltd.

The problem was to build up a circle of reference — taking the modern mind to be the mediaeval mind with wash after wash of classical culture poured over it since the Renaissance. That was the psyche, if you like. One had to deal with one's own subject.

. . . The material one wants to fit in doesn't always work. If the stone isn't hard enough to maintain the form, it has to go out.

[What is to come after *Thrones?*] It is difficult to write a paradiso when all the superficial indications are that you ought to write an apocalypse. It is obviously much easier to find inhabitants for an inferno or even a purgatorio. I am trying to collect the record of the top flights of the mind. I might have done better to put Agassiz on top instead of Confucius.

[T]his is provisionally what I have to do: I must clarify obscurities; I must make clearer definite ideas or dissociations. I must find a verbal formula to combat the rise of brutality — the principle of order versus the split atom. . . .

An epic is a poem containing history. The modern mind contains heteroclite elements. The past epos has succeeded when all or a great many of the answers were assumed, at least between author and audience, or a great mass of audience. . . .

I am writing to resist the view that Europe and civilization are going to Hell. If I am being "crucified for an idea" — that is the coherent idea around which my muddles accumulated — it is probably the idea that European culture ought to survive, that the best qualities of it ought to survive along with whatever other cultures, in whatever universality. Against the propaganda of terror and the propaganda of luxury, have you a nice simple answer? One has worked on certain materials trying to establish bases and axes of reference. In writing so as to be understood, there is always the problem of rectification without giving up what is correct.

[The title] *Rock Drill* was intended to imply the necessary resistance in getting a certain main thesis across — hammering. I was not following the three divisions of the *Divine Comedy* exactly. One can't follow the Dantesquan cosmos in an age of experiment. But I have made the division between people dominated by emotion, people struggling upwards, and those who have some part of the divine vision. The thrones in Dante's *Paradiso* are for the spirits of the people who have been responsible for good government. The thrones in *The Cantos* are an attempt to move out from egoism and to establish some definition of an order possible or at any rate conceivable on earth. One is held up by the low percentage of reason which seems to operate in human affairs. *Thrones* concerns the states of mind of people responsible for something more than their personal conduct.

. . . There is no doubt that the writing is too obscure as it stands, but I hope that the order of ascension in the Paradiso will be toward a greater limpidity.

2. Criticism and Scholarship

Max Halperen

How to Read a Canto

By 1920, Ezra Pound—the stormiest literary hurricane of the twentieth century—had already led many lives: he had passed through a number of poetic phases; he had criticized art, music, literature, and society; he had been and was a "foreign correspondent" for little magazines like *Poetry* and *The Little Review*; he had helped Yeats redirect his poetry and had beaten the drums for Eliot and Joyce; he had translated Provençal and Chinese poetry and Japanese No plays; he had started or touted literary movements like imagism and free verse, and had passed beyond them. And he had a number of other lives to go, several of which would culminate in a decade in St. Elizabeth's—where he continued writing, criticizing, contributing, translating, touting—and trying to help any young poet who would listen.

As a poet, however, this one-man world had already committed himself to the poem that would take the rest of his life and that would integrate or at least incorporate the entire skein of experience and idea that is Ezra Pound. When he began *The Cantos* in 1917, he described it in a letter as a "new long poem (really L O N G, endless, leviathanic)." He could scarcely have known just where his life, and therefore the poem, would lead him, but he certainly was aware of the ambitiousness of his project. It was and remains his major bid for poetic immortality. No wonder, then, that Pound, far from wrapping himself in a cloak of assumed indifference, has expressed concern more than once that his poem be properly understood, and has lashed out bitterly when he felt he was being misunderstood. Yeats thought he was being helpful when, in *A Packet for Ezra Pound*, he repeated what Pound had told him about the fugal nature of the poem. "If Yeats knew a fugue from a frog," Pound told one of his correspondents, "he might have transmitted what I told him in some way that would have helped rather than obfuscated *his* readers." Two years later, Pound was even more exasperated: "God damn Yeats' bloody paragraph. Done more to prevent people from reading Cantos for what is *on the page* than any other smoke screen."

Reprinted from Richard E. Langford and William E. Taylor, eds., *The Twenties, Poetry and Prose: 20 Critical Essays* (Deland, Florida: Everett/Edwards, 1966), pp. 7–13, by permission of the publisher and the author.

"Reading . . . for what is *on the page.*" Is it possible to do so? The smoke screen created by both attackers and defenders of the poem seems thick indeed. "Doubtless," wrote one critic,

> the reader will already have observed that one of the things I have asked of Mr. Watts is that he should be familiar with page 38 of the *ABC of Reading;* for unless the critic happens to know that page, he can scarcely be asked to understand Canto LXXV (though with the hint in line 9 a writer with the ability to read music and a knowledge of fifteenth-century musical symbology might possibly puzzle it out alone).

Thick indeed. And is it possible to read for what is on the page despite the inherent difficulties of the poem itself, seeing it neither as "rambling talk" (Allen Tate) nor as a set of obscure statements that can be understood only in relation to their sources?

I think that with a minimum of help—the sort of help provided by very occasional reference to the *Annotated Index to the Cantos of Ezra Pound* — it is quite possible to read the poem as a poem, provided one gives it the same attention one gives any difficult poem, being alive to the tone of each line, awake to its implications, aware of its context. If that is done, one will find, I think, that documents, translations, descriptions, personal comments — all may be read as images, directly reflecting the poet's state of mind or implying his attitude toward what he is presenting.

The following, then, is an experiment in reading, concentrating on the opening cantos. If the poem is at all ascertainable on its own merits, then surely these cantos are acid tests. Rewritten and re-shuffled, they can scarcely be read as part of a narrative design. Canto I appeared at the end of Canto III in the first published draft. Canto II, with a different opening, was published originally as Canto VIII. Canto VI has been cut to half its original size. Comment that might have explained some of the material has been cut away. Pound himself admitted privately that some of the early material was presented in a manner "perhaps too enigmatically and abreviatedly. I hope, heaven help me, to bring them into some sort of design and architecture later."

As far back as 1912, Pound wrote: "One wants to find out what sort of things endure, and what sort of things are transient; what sort of things recur. . . ." We may take *The Cantos* as the record of Pound's attempt to "find out." It is, then, a quest. And Pound, wishing to indicate something of his own long poetic journey, begins

Canto I with a translation from the *Odyssey* that runs for two pages:

> And then went down to the ship,
> Set keel to breakers, forth on the godly sea. . . .

It is a long journey. [Through dark fog and] over "deepest water," the ship moves on its strange voyage, coming at last to the dread shores of Hades. Odysseus and his men need advice on how to get home, and they have been told that only the ghost of the prophet Tiresias can help them. On the shores of Hades they pray, pour libations, sacrifice sheep. At last Tiresias arrives, drinks the sheep's blood, and tell Odysseus what lies in store for him. Then come the rest of the "impotent dead" to drink the blood, be momentarily revived, and tell their tales.

Suggesting an artistic continuity from Homer's time until now, the ancient epic serves as a gateway to Pound's modern epic, for Pound also is about to set out on a journey through mist and over deep water — though his will be an intellectual journey; and Pound also will attempt to inject blood into the ghosts of the past so that they may speak to and comment on the present. "Nothing is new," Pound wrote in the thirties, "and all good is renewal." In fact, Canto I may be taken as an example of such a renewal, for Pound has translated, not directly from the Greek, but from a Renaissance Latin pony by the Andreas Divus cited at the end of the Canto, and has employed, not modern English, but the " 'Seafarer' metre, or something like it." The implication is that despite (or because of) these transformations, Homer's book of the dead retains its muscle.

But to read the Canto as though it already incorporated or even implied much about the rest of the long poem is, I think, to miss what is on the page. For the moment, the Homeric vision has renewed itself in Pound's mind, as, presumably, it did in Divus'. But after Tiresias speaks, the vision fades, perhaps because of limitations inherent in the material itself — the translation does, after all, suggest a certain remoteness from our own time; or because of limitations in the experience of the poet himself — he does, after all, have a long journey to make. In the *Odyssey*, the prophet's advice is quite detailed, but in Pound's version it is cut to a very brief statement that provides no advice at all. In his search for what is recurrent and what is permanent, this new Odysseus will have no Tiresias to guide him. "Lie quiet Divus," says Pound toward the end of the Canto to the Latin translator of the *Odyssey*. "I mean,

that is, Andreas Divus." The spell is broken. The excitement of
those primitive rituals on the shores of hell has given way to a
matter-of-fact comment. And Odysseus ceases to speak in the
first person:

> And he sailed, by Sirens and thence outward ...

There are, then, to be no guides to the realm of the permanent.
But there are many Scyllas and Charybdises — several of which are
singled out in Cantos II and III.

Though sailing into the past over "deepest water," Pound has
always denied any sentimental yearning for the bygone: "It may
suit some of my friends to go about with their young noses pointing
skyward, decrying the age and comparing us unfavorably to the
dead men of Hellas or of Hesperian Italy ... But I, for one, have no
intention of decreasing my enjoyment of this vale of tears by under-
estimating my own generation." As far as he is concerned, he seeks
only what is permanently alive, or what can be made to live. But
that is scarcely the only concern; there is also the problem of presenting the past in such a way that it, like Tiresias, speaks directly
to the living. For living ideas may easily be stifled by dead forms, by
outmoded styles and methods, by words that do not quite suit the
material, by minds unable to absorb a new viewpoint. Thus, the
need to break old forms and to disrupt old mental grooves, and thus
Pound's concern with it. Precisely that need lies at the heart of
Canto II.

The point is made rather simply in the opening lines of the Canto:

> Hang it all, Robert Browning,
> there can be but the one "Sordello."
> But Sordello, and my Sordello?
> Lo Sordels si fo di Mantovana.

The direct address to Browning suggests a sense of kinship and implies something of an internal struggle — as though Pound had
toyed with the possibility of adapting Browning's method and had,
regretfully, discarded it. It suggests also, I think, something of the
joyous energy flowing into the young poet as he finds it possible —
even necessary — to strike out on his own. Much as he might admire
Sordello — and we have evidence aplenty that he did — Pound cannot simply rewrite the earlier poem either in form or in content. But
Sordello as a person — no longer within quotation marks, and thus
no longer a literary character — can, of course, be used again; there

can be more than one version of the thirteenth-century Italian troubador, and Pound's version, "my Sordello," will necessarily be different from Browning's. Now, as though beginning a fresh appraisal, Pound records the biographical snippet: "the Sordellos came from Mantua."

These lines take us, then, from a fixed form, *Sordello*, to a new form and a fresh look at the source materials. The following lines reverse the order: an ancient image of life and life's energies, the elemental sea itself, is stirred up; however, the result is nothing but a wave running in a beach-groove, reanimating an ancient theme:

> So-shu churned in the sea.
> Seal sports in the spray-whited circles of
>   cliff-wash,
> Sleek head, daughter of Lir,
>   eyes of Picasso
> Under black fur-hood, lithe daughter of
>   Ocean;
> And the wave runs in the beach-groove:
> "Eleanor,

The meaning of these lines is probably clearer in the first version of this Canto, which was prefaced by a rather heavily ironic image of passion and inspiration in bondage to the past:

> Dido chocked up with tears for dead Sichaeus;
> And the weeping Muse, weeping, widowed, and willing,
> The weeping Muse
>   Mourns Homer,
> Mourns the days of long song.

Several lines later Pound tells us that

> Tyro to shoreward lies lithe with Neptunus
> And the glass-clear wave arches over them;
> Seal sports in the spray-whited circles of cliff-wash,
> Sleek head, daughter of Lir, eyes of Picasso

and the rest follows.

Three stages seem to be indicated in the earlier version: farthest out to sea, the sea-god; closer, the circles of cliff-wash; finally, the beach-groove. After the images of weeping Dido and the widowed Muse, the appearance of Neptune indicates a new infusion of elemental energy, possibly a new vision. The present tense implies that

such energy is always present, always recreative. As we move closer
to the shore-line, we see evidence of the creative energies of the sea,
first in a physical embodiment: "Seal sports. . . ." But those energies
are also mental ("sleek head") and artistic ("eyes of Picasso/
Under black furhood"); these too are creatures, "daughters," of the
elemental natural forces represented by the sea god, whether he is
named Lir (Irish) or Ocean (Greek).

And yet, when the fresh spurt of energy comes ashore, when the
creative impulse spends itself, it may well result in nothing more
than the repetition of an old idea, it may move in an old groove —
the theme of destructive beauty. There is renewal here, but of a sort
that deadens instead of enlivening. The Greek epithets describe
Helen as ship- and city-destroying (derived from Aeschylus' *Aga-
memnon* — a fact which may content some but which is quite beside
the point). Eleanor, however, is not simply another Helen; she is, as
Canto VI describes her, also "domna jauzionda," the joyous lady
capable of attracting and encouraging the troubador elite. Thus
Pound restates the need to break old forms and to look at materials
afresh. The beach groove ignores differences; it would lose whatever
is unique in Eleanor.

In the present version of the Canto, So-shu (whose identity has
never been settled) clearly replaces Neptune as the instigator of
fresh power. The shift from Mantua to China in itself suggests an
infusion of new materials and forms. Churning in the sea, So-shu is
in touch with the infinite and the elemental; by stirring, he creates
new combinations. But even his Oriental waves slip into the old
Occidental groove. It is difficult to break an old habit of mind.

The problem is scarcely a new one; it was discerned and described
by Homer. He might have been blind, but his ear was precise, his
technique certain:

> And poor old Homer blind, blind as a
> bat,
> Ear, ear for the sea-surge, murmur of
> old men's voices.

He could fix both the surge of new energies already noted in the
Canto and the fears of old men. We are given the speech of the
elders of Troy as they watch Helen on the wall:

> Moves, yes she moves like a goddess
> And has the face of a god
>
> .   .   .   .

> And doom goes with her in walking,
> Let her go back to the ships.

This, of course, is another version of the beach-groove. Beyond, the sea's energies forever enter man:

> And by the beach-run, Tyro
> Twisted arms of the sea-god,
> Lithe sinews of water ...

But on the beach no new groove is carved; there is only a "Quiet sun-tawny sand-stretch."

Even the assurance and energy provided by the vision of a god may be lost. It is possible to be certain of an immortal truth, yet be unable to convince others. In fact, a group faced with the same experience may see it quite differently from the one perspective visionary. In Canto II, the god Bacchus appears to a sea-captain. Far more than Ovid, the source of the tale, Pound stresses the certainty of the vision. Twice the captain repeats:

> I have seen what I have seen.

He insists:

> Aye, I, Acoetes, stood there,
> and the god stood by me,

and again:

> When they brought the boy I said:
> "He has a god in him,
> though I do not know which god."
> And they kicked me into the fore-stays.

The last line quoted indicates the connection between this episode and the rest of the Canto. Acoetes sees the god, but none of his men do. King Pentheus of Thebes, to whom Acoetes tells his story, refuses to believe it. And the Canto fades out into a world, not of certainty, but of instability:

> The tower like a one-eyed great goose
> cranes up out of the olive-grove.

The instability of the world in which the poet seeks the recurrent and the permanent — this seems to be the central theme of Canto

III. On the slither of time the poet must seek the eternal — the gods. In an early draft of the first Canto, Pound wrote:

> And shall I claim;
> Confuse my own phantastikon,
> Or say the filmy shell that circumscribes me
> Contains the actual sun;
>   Confuse the thing I see
> With actual gods behind me?

At the opening of Canto III, Pound describes himself as a young and impecunius aesthete, alone and idle in Venice:

> I sat on the Dogana's steps
> For the gondolas cost too much, that
>   year,
> And there were not "those girls," there
>   was one face,
> And the Buccentoro twenty yards off,
>   howling "Stretti,"
> And the lit cross-beams, that year, in the
>   Morosini.

The repetition of "that year" calls attention, here as elsewhere, to the temporal and impermanent nature of these experiences, while the third line suggests their personal, accidental quality (if one is diligent and devoted to such matters, one may trace "those girls" to Browning; but Pound expunged Browning from the passage and I see little reason to insist on writing him back in; the line stands as a statement about two different experiences and that is what matters). But against these fragmentary experiences, Pound places an image of the gods, who — representing immortal truth and immortal vigor — are ever-present:

> Gods float in the azure air,
> Bright gods and Tuscan, back before
>   dew was shed.
> Light: and the first light, before ever
>   dew was fallen.

They are presented as an idle young aesthete might see them or intuit them: beautiful but unrelated to the world of men. Upon entering that active world — as Pound does through the tale of the Cid —

> My Cid rode up to Burgos,
> Up to the studded gate between two towers,

one finds it difficult to engage the gods; one finds not eternity but death and destruction:

> Ignez da Castro murdered, and a wall
> Here stripped, here made to stand.
> Drear waste. . .

In Canto IV Pound asserts the method, already implied in a number of places, by which he hopes to overcome time and change. Joining and juxtaposing images, he outlines, in a tentative way, several recurrent attitudes. He also asserts — and this too has been implied — that it is not enough for the poet to discover what recurs and what endures. Odysseus may return with the wisdom of the prophet, but loses all companions. Acoetes is firm — "I have seen what I have seen"—but he is the only one to see it and is destroyed. The artist's knowledge must somehow be related to the active world of men. Otherwise, as Pound has never tired of insisting, such knowledge is useless.

Recalling the end of Canto III, Canto IV opens with the destructive vision that animated Homer's pen:

> Palace in smoky light,
> Troy but a heap of smouldering boundary
> stones.

But as the artist who would preserve rather than destroy, and who is concerned with the vision and the spirit that can animate an entire community, Pound appeals:

> ANAXIFORMINGES! Aurunculeia!
> Hear me. Cadmus of Golden Prows!
> The silver mirrors catch the bright stones
> and flare,
> Dawn, to our waking, drifts in the green
> cool light;
> Dew-haze blurs, in the grass, pale ankles
> moving.
> Beat, beat, whirr, thud, in the soft turf
> under the apple trees,
> Choros nympharum, goat-foot, with the
> pale foot alternate.

"Anaxiforminges" — "ruling the lyre" — opens Pindar's second
Olympian Ode, and suggests a community event in celebration of
the gods; Aurunculeia is the bride in whose honor Catullus wrote his
wedding song, another ceremonial at whose center is the god of marriage; Cadmus is, of course, the legendary founder of Thebes. All
suggest communal enterprise centered in communal belief. They are
presented too cryptically, perhaps, but the very brevity of these
allusions indicates, I should think, that Pound has not discovered in
these earlier suggestions very useful guides for his purpose. His
mind slips from these fragments to the reality of an ever-present
dawn alight with creative vigour; and in the dance of nymphs and
fauns there is a suggestion of joy and freedom expressed, though not
confined by, the pattern of the dance. The pattern implied by
Pindar can be but a pallid reflection of this dance.

In sharp contrast to the imagery of "green cool light" and "pale
ankles moving," we are shown an old man "by the curved, carved
foot of the couch." Like the old man of Troy, he will speak of doom,
and we may expect the "beach-groove" of Canto II to be explored,
as indeed it is, with allusions to the dark stories of Tereus' passion
and the destruction of Acteon, and with suggestions of their Provençal counterparts: the wave of renewal and recurrence runs in the
beach-groove. The first half of the canto focuses on a vision of Diana
at her bath, a vision that includes both a sense of ecstasy and a
sense of mystery:

> Not a ray, not a slivver, not a spare disc
>   of sunlight
> Flaking the black, soft water;
> Bathing the body of nymphs, of nymphs,
>   and Diana,
> Nymphs, white-gathered about her, and
>   the air, air,
> Shaking, air alight with the goddess,
>   fanning their hair in the dark.

Out of such a vision emerges poetic energy and productivity, but,
for the community at large, the will to secrecy may be destructive
of whatever is fine and innocent:

> And she went toward the window,
>   the slim white stone bar
> Making a double arch;
> Firm even fingers held to the firm pale
>   stone;
> Swung for a moment...

But there is another way in which the gods may manifest themselves: publicly and communally, by the light of the sun:

> The liquid and rushing crystal
>   beneath the knees of the gods.
> Ply over ply, thin glitter of water;
> Brook film bearing white petals.
> The pines at Takasago
>   grow with the pines of Ise!

"Ply over ply" indicates Pound's attempt to see through cultural
levels for what recurs. In reaching around the globe for his imagery
of order Pound is, of course, preparing the way for the Confucian
and Chinese Cantos, and he is suggesting as well that the East provides a necessary counterpart or corrective for the basic patterns of
the West. He returns briefly to Catullus' wedding song and makes
it a reflection of the "Choros nympharum": "Blue agate casing the
sky" recalling "the green cool light"; "saffron sandal so petals the
narrow foot" recalling the "pale ankles moving." Here is recurrence, though scarcely a very exact one.

But between what the artist perceives—such perceptions as Pound
is currently piecing together—and the spirit that drives the community, there ought, Pound insists, to be some correlation. That is
the note on which the Canto closes.

Canto VI restates the problem in a new guise. A group, "we," is
opposed to the one, "you." The many may know what the one has
done, for action is readily perceivable. "We" may also know what
Guillaume, one of the founders of the troubador tradition, has done.
These are fairly public matters:

> What you have done, Odysseus,
>   We know what you have done . . .
> And that Guillaume sold out his ground
>   rents
> (Seventh of Poitiers, Ninth of Aquitain).
> "Tant las fotei com auzirets
> "Cen e quatre vingt et veit vetz. . . ."
> The stone is alive in my hand, the crops
>   will be thick in my death-year. . .

But as the following lines indicate, there are mysteries to which the
many, though having access to common knowledge, do not possess
the key—that of language, for example, and that of sensitivity. The
Provençal couplet stands for precisely what it is — something most

of us will not understand and a sense of pagan joy our society has
dispensed with ("I copulated with them as you shall hear/One
hundred and eighty-eight times"). The next two lines suggest the
perception of the one, the artist perhaps, capable of sensing the
spirit in what otherwise would be dead matter. Like the Greek gods,
the spirit is universal and immortal, and the artist to whom the
stone is alive may, like an ancient demigod, bring the wasteland to
life. The line also suggests that there is a connection between the
artist's perception and the health of the land—a point Pound will
make time and again in the course of *The Cantos*—and it suggests
further the possibility of combining perception and power in one
man — another idea that Pound will harp on in the course of his
long poem.

The transmission of such perception depends, as the poem has
already suggested, on receptive mentalities. They are not easy to
find. Eleanor is of the line of Guillaume, and we meet her later in
the Canto as the "joyous lady" of the troubadors. But then "Louis
is wed with Eleanor," and a new, unperceiving mentality is intro-
duced. To Louis, the line of Guillaume has nothing to do with the
poetic and the spiritual; it is purely political:

> And had (He, Guillaume) a son that
>   had to wife
> The Duchess of Normandia whose
>   daughter
> Was wife to King Henry e maire del
>   rei jove. . .

The spirit of the Odyssean voyage, as Pound defined it in Canto I,
has nothing to do with Louis' crusade:

> Went over sea till day's end (he, Louis,
>   with Eleanor).

The first half of the line is derived from the translation in Canto I,
while the second half recalls the foolishly pedantic "He, Guillaume."
We are in different mental worlds, though in the same physical
ambience.

The spirit in the stone is a mystery. But even public documents
may hide the truth to the artist who is not willing to play the part
of historian. After taking us through the divorce between Louis and
Eleanor and the marriage of Eleanor and Henry II, Pound presents
a wedding agreement:

> Nauphal, Vexis, Harry joven
> In pledge for all his life and life of all
>   his heirs
> Shall have Gisors, and Vexis, Neufchastel
> But if no issue Gisors shall revert . . .

Here as elsewhere the ellipsis is intended to suggest a good deal that remains unstated — for, as an earlier version of Canto VI reports at great length, Harry joven, Henry II's heir, died before the wedding, but Henry steadfastly refused to return Gisors. Another agreement follows, one between Richard III and Philip of France:

> "Need not wed Alix . . . in the name
> Trinity holy indivisible . . . Richard our
>   brother.

Again the dots hide a good deal; the simple fact that something has been left out is all that Pound wishes to indicate here; it is not terribly important to note that the agreement was signed in an atmosphere of ungodly hate that scarcely warrants the references to the Trinity and to "our brother."

But when one has all the facts, both documents and poems may, if properly aligned, prove useful in shaping the form of a recurrent mood or idea. At long last the fact that Sordello came from around Mantua is to be given a place in the story—as part of an emerging idea or spirit, linked to another fact and thus suggesting that Pound may have something solid to work with. Bernart de Ventadorn sings of his lady as one who, like Diana, "sheds such light in the air." But, concerned with the spirit, not with private possession of the beloved, Bernart asks:

> "Send word I ask you to Eblis
>   you have seen that maker
> "And finder of songs so far afield as this
> "That he may free her,
>   who sheds such light in the air."

It is now that Pound returns us to Sordello:

> E lo Sordels si fo di Mantovana,
> Son of a poor knight, Sier Escort,
> And he delighted himself in chançons
> And mixed with the men of the court

> And went to the court of Richard Saint
>   Boniface
> And was there taken with love for his
>   wife Cunizza, da Romano,
> That freed her slaves on a Wednesday
> Masnatas et servos, witness.

This Sordello is one who recognizes in others such as Cunizza the same freedom of spirit he possesses himself; Sordello's biography and Cunizza's testament reveal the same order of mind as Bernart's. A new groove begins to be shaped.

The discussion above is scarcely designed to prove that everything in Pound's long poem is self-evident. That cryptic passage at the opening of Canto IV is enough to bury any such nonsense, and it takes only a glance at the rest of the poem to discern many such passages. But whatever source-hunting is needed to clarify an allusion, the reader's first task is to ascertain its force and meaning in *The Cantos*, not its position in the source. In fact, anyone who has read carefully both *The Cantos* and Pound's major sources—Pére de Mailla's multi-volume history of China, for example, or the collected works of John Adams — must conclude, I think, that the sources are often beside the point, and often misleading. Only "on the page" can we discover Pound's intentions. Only "on the page" do we find, if we look closely, a carefully designed set of themes and variations for each Canto — themes and variations usually announced at the opening of the Canto.

Perhaps — and one must confess to a certain wistfulness at this point — if the poem acquires enough readers who are willing to read the poem, not poetry-substitutes, it may become possible to assess it sanely and meaningfully, saving it from both the Pound cult and the anti-Pound cult.

Hugh Kenner

Leucothea's Bikini: Mimetic Homage

Pound's characteristic act — the running paraphrase, the torqued translation, the quick skim of his light across glints hidden to any blander gaze at alien surfaces — goes unnoticed by the terminology he has himself furnished to criticism, and so gets dismissed as idiosyncrasy, intruding into occasions for pure contemplation. The man who rendered an ideogram as "bigosh" seems not to be following the ideogrammic method, which entails (does it not?) a selfless interaction of nodal things, quirkiness subsumed in oriental calm. For ideograms, images, the right hand on the chisel, these belong to a poetic of objects; we assume perhaps too readily that a poem is like a statue, too tardily that it is like a drama, a drama enacted in time, before our minds, by the single actor, its maker.

"Imitation, then, being natural to us," wrote Aristotle, "as also the sense of harmony and rhythm, the meters being obviously species of rhythms, it was through their original aptitude, and by a series of improvements for the most part gradual on their first efforts, that they created poetry out of their improvisation." To see in a poem a poetic act is to see gestures of a performer, not incongruities in a statue. Consider Leucothea's bikini.

> That the wave crashed, whirling the raft, then
> Tearing the oar from his hand,
>   broke mast and yard-arm
> And he was drawn down under the wave,
>   The wind tossing,
> Notus, Boreas,
>   as it were thistle-down.
> Then Leucothea had pity,
>   "mortal once
> Who now is a sea-god:
>   *nostou*
> *gaies Phaiēkōn*, . . ."[1]

Reprinted from Noel Stock, ed., *Ezra Pound — Perspectives: Essays in Honor of His Eightieth Birthday* (Chicago: Henry Regnery, 1965), pp. 25-40, by permission of The Sterling Lord Agency. Copyright 1965 by Henry Regnery.
[1]I am transliterating all Greek, for the reader's comfort and the printer's.

21

So closes "Canto XCV," each phrase excerpted in sequence from the fifth book of the *Odyssey*, lines 313-45. The typography not only guides the voice, but manages to suggest that the Homeric page has been ventilated by simply underlining phrases. The last three words draw us down into the Greek itself, and the next Canto (the first in *Thrones*) opens with another Greek word, Leucothea's next contribution, before rising back into English as she slips into the water:

> *Krēdemnon . . .*
> *krēdemnon . . .*
> and the wave concealed her,
>   dark mass of great water.

This is the black wave, *melan kyma,* into which she disappears at line 353; with her disappearance Pound's dealings with the episode cease. The one obscurity in this brilliantly selective paraphrase is *krēdemnon,* for which there happens not to be a simple English equivalent. Pound offered his gloss a page earlier:

> "My bikini is worth yr/raft". Said Leucothoe

She said something to this effect when she gave Odysseus her *krēdemnon,* the word Pound writes twice because it occurs twice in the Greek, when she offers it (346) and when she hands it over (351). Can it really be an Argive bikini? It is the magic garment that he is to spread under his chest till he gets to land, *"phylaktērion thatlattiou kakou,* a protector against evil seas," writes one scholiast and *"hōsper symbalon tēs theias boētheias,* as a token of divine assistance," writes another, pointlessly explicit. Liddell and Scott are more helpful: "It seems to have been a sort of *veil* or *mantilla with lappets,* passing over the head and hanging down on each side, so that at pleasure it might be drawn over the face." Andromache, Juno and Penelope all wear one, so it is "mostly therefore worn by persons of rank," though in *Odyssey* vi, 100 Nausikaa's waiting-women toss off their *krēdemna* before playing ball. Whether or not it generally connotes rank, there is not doubt that it is a covering for the head; indeed, the word is metaphorically applied to "the battlements which top and crown a city's walls," and in both the *Iliad* and the *Odyssey* we find *Troiēs hiera krēdemna,* the sacred battlements of Troy. Though it isn't Homer's usual word for battlements, this metaphor can eliminate any lingering doubt that *krēdemnon* is associated with the head; and the trouble Pound has taken to write out the Greek word twice, at a point of maximum emphasis, suggests that he would have glanced at what Liddell and Scott have to say about it.

So why did the *krēdemnon* become a bikini? For several reasons; the first is the need for some remotely plausible equivalent for a word on which Liddell and Scott expended a paragraph. With tiller and yardarm gone, the raft a shuttlecock for wind gods, Poseidon Earthshaker rearing up great black waves, are we to pause for an archaeological footnote about the costumes of Greek ladies? Or to wonder why a sea nymph's costume includes something to put on her head? Something, moreover, with strings to tie it shut across her face? A miraculous garment is what the story requires, a miraculous garment wearable at sea.

This kind of difficulty has on other occasions pressed Pound to some of his most characteristic ingenuities. In "The Seafarer," for instance, we read

Dagas sind gewitene
ealle onmedlan   eorthan rices

— days are departed, all the glory of earthly realms. Here Pound, having written "Days little durable," was brought up short, we may suppose, by the problem of an equivalent for *rices*; for though the "Seafarer" sensibility remains imbedded in the ninth century, words like *realms* and *kingdoms* have gone on acquiring sophisticated connotations. The king or Caesar of "The Seafarer" ("nearon nu cyningas ne caseras / ne goldgiefan. . .") is no more than the gold-giver, the personal overlord, at most the tribal head. A *kingdom*, on the other hand, is a political organization of some complexity, and *realm* is touched with the sumptuousness of *royaume*. In this difficulty the mere look of *rices* seems to have suggested a usable noun; whereupon the need for assonance supplied a stand-in for *onmedlan*, and *eorthan*, as though in response to the tug of the Anglo-Saxon words, became not earthly but earthen:

And all arrogance of earthen riches.

Riches for *rices*, like some of the details in *Sextus Propertius*, has ever since suggested to suspicious minds a mistranslation; but no one has suggested anything better. It remains a plausible word in the modern poem, and a modern poem is what is being generated.

For Pound (this brings us to the second principle) exacts of his words that they sit easily on modern tongues, and moreover that

we shall be aware of this fact. "The Seafarer" ensures our awareness by its very existence as a *tour de force*; only detailed comparison with the original will uncover the instances when the "correct"
word has been replaced by the word that fits today. Elsewhere he
is determined to hold before our minds a fact easily forgotten: that
if, as Wyndham Lewis once put it, whole landslides from other times
and tongues are coming onto his pages, it is into the twentieth
century that they are sliding, at the bidding of a twentieth-century
poet. The bikini of Leucothea, like the Frigidaire he imagined
Sextus Propertius disclaiming, is precisely the contemporary note,
both the shock of a reality beyond normal imaginative reality, and
the stubborn reminder that transposition, not recreation, is going
on, that the mind remains anchored in these times, not those.

For he is not an illusionist: his aesthetic is older, more catholic,
than Ibsen's. As Shakespeare, suspending the miracle, bids us remember that before our eyes on the stage "some squeaking Cleo-
patra," a boy-Cleopatra, is miming "the posture of a whore," so
Pound does not offer the flawless miraculous product but drama-
tizes an imaginative process.

The process is easily seen in the China Cantos, where we find,
superimposed, three things: (1) a bare high chronicle manner moving to the clash of oriental cymbals and drums, paraphrase of some
dynastic record that does not exist, being generated in (2) the
imagination of an American who is (3) exiled in twentieth-century
Italy and leafing through a multi-volumed history[2] published in
eighteenth-century France. In "Canto LVI" all these elements are
readily separable.

> Slept on the pine needle carpet
>   sprinkled horse blood
> praying no brave man be born among Mongols

— that is the chronicle.

> Billets, biglietti, as coin was too heavy for transport
>   but redeemed the stuff at one third
>
> And Ou-Kiai had another swat at the tartars
>   and licked 'em

— that is the American paraphraser, in Italy.

> HONG VOU voyant ses forces affoiblir
>   dict: Que la vertu t'inspire, Tchu-ouen.

---

[2]*Histoire Générale de la Chine, ou Annales de cet Empire*, traduites du Tong-
Kien-Kang-Mou, par le feu père Joheph Anne-Marie de Moyriac de Mailla,
Paris, 1777-83, 12 vol. Hereafter cited as Mailla.

— that is his French book.

The whole being meant to wear this look of rapid resourceful paraphrase, Pound followed the appropriate method, which was to work through the French volumes setting down rough metrical gists in a notebook, and then preserve the notebook form — marginal dates, page references, colloquial comments — in the text that went to the printer. Thus on page 459 of the second volume of Mailla he read this paragraph:

> Hiang-yu étoit né avec un goût décidé pour le commandement, & il ne put jamais faire le moindre progrès dans les lettres, aux- quelles d'abord il avoit été destiné, & qui n'étoient utiles, disoit-il, qu'a transmettre des noms à la postérité. Il ne montra pas moins de répugnance lorsqu'on voulut lui apprendre à faire des armes, qui ne le mettoient en état que de résister à un seul homme; mais il n'en fut pas de même de l'art qui enseigne à en vaincre dix mille, dans lequel il fit les plus grands progrès. Hiang-yu avoit huit pieds de haut, & il joignoit à cette taille avantageuse une force extraordi- naire de corps; mais d'ailleurs il étoit audacieux, cruel, fier, & de mauvaise foi.

After underlining "à transmettre des noms à la postérité" and mak- ing marginal pencil slashes at three other points, he sketched in a large paper-bound book labelled "Vols 1-2 Mailla"[3] this paraphrase:

```
Hiang-yu
    with a taste
    for commanding
        made no progress
            in letters
useful only he said
    to transmit names to
            posterity
neither wd he learn fencing —
    but thought in terms
        of 10 000s
  — a giant
        who kept no
            faith
Dam'd Rhoosian
    if you ask
        me
              p. 459
```

[3] I am indebted to the Princess Mary de Rachewiltz for permitting me to in- spect this notebook, now at Brunnenburg.

LIBRARY
College of St. Francis
JOLIET, ILL.

66321

This is lively, like a Constable sketch. In the final text the emphases are diminished in keeping with Hiang-yu's minor role in "Canto LIV":

> Now after the end of EULH and the death of his eunuch
> were Lieou-pang, and Hiang-yu
>   who had taste for commanding
> but made no progress in letters,
>   saying they serve only to transmit names to posterity
> and he wished to carve up the empire
>   bloody rhooshun, thought in ten thousands
> his word was worth nothing, he would not learn fencing.
>   And
>   against him . . . .

Mailla is present in a certain decorum of phrasing and in the spelling of the proper name; as a headnote to the American printing of the sequence reminds us, "I mostly use the French form." The contemporary American asserts himself in "bloody rhooshun," the chronicle in

>   thought in ten thousands
>   his word was worth nothing.

Modern Italy, except in the persistent concern with the taxonomy of strong men, is barely noticeable.

But the modern Italian setting is always present, shaping the selections and the phrases. Sometimes Pound will abandon all apparent decorum for the sake of keeping before the reader's mind the time in which this work is being done. One day in 1938 (Anno XVI) he had been condensing from Mailla the account of Han Sieun receiving the Tartar King. In "Canto LIV" this receives two-thirds of a page, concluding:

> And the next day two imperial princes went to the Prince
>   Tartar
> the Tchen-yu and brought him to the audience hall
>   where all princes sat in their orders
>   and the Tchen-yu knelt to HAN SIEUN
> and stayed three days there in festival
>   whereafter he returned to his border and province.

Having gotten that far, Pound went to the movies,[4] where a newsreel displayed certain festivals in honor of the visit to Italy of the

---

[4] I owe this information to Mr. John Reid, was was in Rapallo at the time.

modern Tartar King, Adolf Hitler. In the Bay of Naples a squadron of submarines all dived, then surfaced simultaneously. Pound's old friend Ubaldo degli Uberti, who had been a submarine commander in World War I, pronounced such a maneuver very dangerous.[5] That night Pound noted the incident opposite the Tartar King material in his Mailla notebook, with a large swastika as mnemonic of the occasion; and in the text of "Canto LIV" we read:

> (Pretty manoeuvre but the technicians
> watched with their hair standing on end
> anno sixteen, Bay of Naples)

The next item, by contrast, is dated in the margin "B.C. 49." The subject-rhyme, between Hitler's visit and the Tartar King's, has, alas, been obscured to invisibility. But "anno sixteen" retains its function; we are to recall, continually, the time when these pages were written, different from, yet in some ways possibly like, the time they were written about, and keep alert for present relevance.

We are to stay aware, in short, of a performance by a man in a particular place and time, in the presence of particular ancient models: a *mimetic homage*, shaped by person and circumstance, and not at all what is usually meant by translation or transcription. The man is what he is, or what he characterizes himself as being. The time and place guide him constantly; they are his actuality, and he is as responsible to them as to the model. The model may supply enduring ideas or enduring perception, or it may supply no more than a norm of style, as when

> Basinio left greek tags in his margin
> moulding the cadence[6]

Constantly adjusting, in his mimetic homages, the tensions of model, man and circumstance, while never allowing one of them to disappear wholly, he effects and defines the Poundian Art of Translation; for translation, once this principle is understood, becomes merely a special case of the act of writing. We can write nothing except with reference to what has been written before, if only because we cannot set down two words without stirring a whole

---

[5] Information from Mrs. Dorothy Pound.
[6] "Canto CIV." Cf. *The ABC of Reading* (New York: New Directions, 1951), p. 48: "In the margins of his Latin narrative [*Issottaeus*, a poem about Sigismondo Malatesta's love for Isotta] you can still see the tags of Homer that he was using to keep his melodic sense active."

language into life. We can write nothing except as we, whoever we may be, write it. And we cannot possibly write except here and now, and because here and now what we write seems for some reason worth the writing. Translation seems to have worried no one in the eighteenth century, when the principles of mimetic homage were still understood: a man who thought in couplets fetched from Greek what his age could use, moral exempla. It worried everyone in the nineteenth century, when, under the influence of the Holy Spirit theory, men came to hold, for the first time, that poetry at least is untranslatable; for the original poem is testimony to the moment when the Holy Spirit seized its author, an event not to be counterfeited. Having had the nerve to translate poetry in the face of this prohibition, Pound has, not unnaturally, incurred considerable abuse.

The abuse bases itself on the cult of the dictionary, an eighteenth-century invention which came to inhibit everyone by suggesting that languages were systems of equivalences. Matthew Arnold, who had the courage to examine the criteria for translating Homer in a time when such an enterprise seemed virtually impossible, was driven to posit as a norm the response of the Professor of Greek at Oxford; that translation will have succeeded, he said, which the Professor of Greek concedes has aroused in him an experience comparable to that aroused by the original. The Professor of Greek is of course a walking dictionary, his mind stuffed with Greek-English near-equivalences. Even as Arnold wrote, Liddell and Scott were cataloguing these equivalences, at Oxford, imperishably. There is really no hope of satisfying the Professor of Greek, for whom a *kredemnon* (complete with half a column of footnotes) is something a woman of status puts on her head, *and* for whom the line

> *tē de, tode krēdemnon hypo sternoio tanussai*
> *ambroton*

has irreplaceable rhythmic authority, *and* for whom Odysseus and Leucothea exist at a certain inaccessible, "Hellenic," elevation. No one, except for a line or two at a time, can hope to get all those elements into English at once; and whatever element is lacking at a given instant will draw down the Professor of Greek's reproof: however pretty, not Homer.

Such difficulties are not removed, merely displaced, by the post-Arnoldian fashion of calling a poem an object, and its translation (abandoning moment-by-moment equivalence) a similar object.

Each object is made of dictionary words, analyzable rhythms, identifiable systems of reference. If this fashion permits the details of each object to be referred to its own linguistic system (thus accommodating, for instance, Pound's objection that inflected and uninflected languages take different handling), it makes the question of similarity between model and translation insoluble except by way of (1) dictionary equivalences or (2) local analogies of rhetoric. What fails the former test must either be excused by the latter or dismissed as a mistake. And two elements in the three-way tension of performance are simply ignored: the person and the occasion. All attention shuttles between Original Object and Translated Object. Nobody made either object, and it was made under no circumstances in particular, but rests on our soil like a meteorite, incongruous.

Restore the person, restore the occasion, and we can talk sense. Here is the Greek, or the Latin, or the Chinese; someone like and unlike us wrote it in a time like and unlike ours. It can be read, if not by us, by someone. Here is on the other hand a somewhat similar English poem. It is the printed record of a *performance*, a mimetic homage rendered by a certain man, not concealing his traces, who in his own place and time was moved (why?) to pay in this manner his tribute to a former mastery. We are satisfied if he is true to himself and his time, and shows us that the model is one of the things that he knows, and on this occasion the preponderant thing: preponderant because relevant to what he feels and thinks here and now. He is not archaeologizing, and *bikini*, a live term in his mind now, will do for *krēdemnon*.

And translation, we have said, is a special case only. All writing rewrites what has been written, proceeds according to norms and models, chooses them, fulfills or modifies them, and does these things (if we are aware) in plain sight. Hugh Selwyn Mauberley, when he wrote his one extant poem, was sensitized to Flaubertian propaganda, half-understood. His mind, moreover, reached for analogies to the *objets d'art* among which he had spent his most alert hours; and recollecting in tranquillity the singing of Raymonde Collignon, he set down

Luini in porcelain!

— a visual equation; and

The sleek head emerges
From the gold-yellow frock

As Anadyomene in the opening
Pages of Reinach

— another visual equation, defining not only his subject but himself and his time, his taste for art books and the British Museum Reading Room, from which his imagination is moved to bring forth its choicest treasures. His is a static homage, a *collage* of optical analogies, the rhythm tense, cluttered with hesitations, as the mind picks its careful way among scholarly exactitudes, assembling, precisely, objects into an object, grotesque (amid its pathos) as Benin statuary.

And the contrasting homage is that of "E.P.," who commences by calling it "Envoi," invoking so the presence of Chaucer and Cavalcanti, the Chaucer of the *Troilus* and the Cavalcanti of the *Ballate*. Though the poem as it rests on the page has the look of a *ballata*, and owes Cavalcanti some of its rhythmic deftness, most of the short lines turn out to be halves of iambic pentameters, the traditional English formal measure, and the opening words vary Chaucer's:

Go, dumb-born book

Chaucer had sent forth a "litel" book, no doubt smiling as he reflected on its great length. Pound's "dumb-born" does not smile but is equally indirect. All books are dumb until a voice gives them life. This book, in fact "litel," a mere affair of twelve short poems, is as "dumb" as its contemporary subject: a new attempt, vain, people will say, "to resuscitate the dead art / Of poetry," in a time of Brennbaums, Nixons and *muflisme*.

Tell her that sang me once that song of Lawes:

The dumb thing is charged with telling; books can do that. And a new echo stirs into life:

Go, lovely Rose,
Tell her that wastes her time and me . . .

Roses too are dumb, though lovelier than books; Waller's poem, the very song, in Lawes's setting, that Pound's lady has been singing, specifies the mimetic homage his rose is to perform: blushing, opening ("bid her come forth"), dying, in admonition to inaccessible beauty.

Waller, the rose and the lady live on in the song, reborn as often as it is sung. Pound's book offers to build longevity for the most transient glories, those of a voice.

> Tell her that sheds
> Such treasure in the air,
> Recking naught else but that her graces give
> Life to the moment,
> I would bid them live
> As roses might, in magic amber laid,
> Red overwrought with orange and all made
> One substance and one colour
> Braving time.

In six pentameter lines printed as nine, the caesurae bringing out a precarious beauty, the great Renaissance boast, the Shakespearean boast ("braving time") is reenacted in twentieth-century London, defying earlier moods of the dumb-born book, with its "tawdry cheapness" that shall "outlast our days," and its dismissal, in Establishment accents, of attempts "to maintain 'the sublime' / in the old sense." The sublime is taking form before our ears, in a time so far declined from Waller's that the lady singing Waller's song does not know his name.

As Chaucer sent a book, and Waller a rose, so Pound once more sends a book, containing an ambered rose and terminating in a song which, one day sung, may reenact this moment for new "worshippers" as this moment reenacts so many moments gone. This art of the mimetic homage, located in time and place and stirring to new life models that will not die, is the central Poundian act. It divides itself sharply from Mauberley's "Medallion," the small carved thing exquisite but voiceless, exposed to vicissitudes of taste and cut off from the reality it would celebrate by insisting on visual analogies in the presence of auditory fact. The poesis of objects strikes out after a specious immortality, like Ignez de Castro's,

> Seated there,
>   dead eyes,
> Dead hair under the crown.

Homage by mimesis, the act of a living man, as often as it is repeated, can bring life.

Pound, Joyce, and Flaubert: The Odysseans

In the first versions of *The Cantos,* probably begun in 1911 or 1912 and under intense composition in 1915, Ezra Pound projected the speaker of his poem, himself, as a Dantean visionary in the act of seeking what he defined in his first canto (later discarded) as a 'rag-bag' for the modern world 'to stuff all it's thought in'. His subject was the modern mind, his guide was Robert Browning, his model was Browning's *Sordello,* and the structure of his 'new form', a version of Browning's 'meditative, semi-dramatic, semi-epic story', would 'follow the builder's whim'.[1] The choice of Browning reflected his belief in 1915 that *Sordello* was the last great poetic narrative, itself Browning's version of the 'personal epic', the post-romantic autobiographical poem which at the tame time sought the objective validity of actual history. But by 1922, having completed eight cantos, Pound had lost confidence in the form of his 'rag-bag'. He wrote to his father at the end of 1919 'done cantos 5, 6, 7, each more incomprehensible than the one preceding it; don't know what's to be done about it' (letter at Yale). In 1920 and 1921 he wrote an eighth canto; but, opening as it did with a lament for the passing of the Homeric epic of adventurous deeds, it continued to reflect his uncertainty. In 1923, however, Pound rejected most of old Cantos I–III, especially those parts which were based on Browning. He moved the Odyssey translation from the end of old Canto III to make a new Canto I. Old Canto VIII, with a new introduction that rejects Browning, was moved forward to become Canto II. A new Canto III was made up from fragments of the rejected cantos. Cantos IV–VII were retained substantially the same as the present

---

From Eva Hesse, ed., *New Approaches to Ezra Pound. A Co-ordinated Investigation of Pound's Poetry and Ideas* (Berkeley: University of California, 1969), pp. 125-44. Originally published by the University of California Press; reprinted by permission of The Regents of the University of California and Forrest Read.

[1] The above quotations are from old Canto I (*Poetry,* June 1917), discarded in 1923.

versions.[2] By these revisions Homer became Pound's guide, Aphrodite his muse, and Odysseus his central figure; instead of being merely evocations of past literature, past persons, and past places, reflected in the mind, the poem was now motivated by the fictional pattern of a voyage, by encounters with the living and the dead, and by a traditional epic idea, the *nostos* (the return home).

From the time he arrived in London in 1908, intent on writing an epic poem, Pound's own life had seemed to him an Odyssean adventure and his studies of the past his 'background'. In a 1909 letter to his mother about the feasibility of a modern epic (at Yale), he thought of Homer's Odyssey as a primary model, though at the time Whitman's and Dante's overt use of themselves as epic figures seemed more adaptable. From the beginning, in his essays and reviews, he compares the modern experimental writer to an Odyssean adventurer into the unknown. In his poems the voyage with Homeric echoes of exile and discovery crops up incessantly. His first 'major persona' was 'The Seafarer'; he republished 'The Seafarer' in *Cathay*, (1915), juxtaposing it to his second major persona, 'The Exile's Letter'. In 1906 he had bought Andreas Divus's translation of Homer; in 1909 or 1920 he had conceived the Nekuia as a symbol of his own voyage to Europe; between 1911 and 1914 he had translated the Odyssey passage of Canto I into 'Seafarer' metres; in 1915 he incorporated it into the original third canto. It is only natural, then, that the Odyssey is one of the formative patterns of *Hugh Selwyn Mauberley*, his summary of his London years.

But if the Odyssey was so pervasive as a pattern for his own life and as a pattern of literary form, why did Pound wait so long before making Odysseus the major figure of *The Cantos*? One reason was that his conception changed after 1919: *The Cantos* was to be not a poem written from within modern civilization, but a poem about a break with modern civilization and a search for a new basis. This 'break' is reflected in his personal life, in *Mauberley*, and in Canto VII; it became for him a theory of history, of which the *nostos* is a symbol. Another reason lies in Pound's conception of epic as 'a poem containing history'. A modern epic had to build

---

[2]Publication of the 'old' Cantos I-III, *Poetry*, June-August 1917 (condensed somewhat for *Lustra*, American edition, 1917); IV, Ovid Press, 1919; IV-VII, *Poems* 1918-21 (1921); VIII, *Dial*, May 1922. Myles Slatin describes the history of composition leading up to *A Draft XVI Cantos* (1925) in 'A History of Pound's *Cantos I-XVI*, 1915-1925', *American Literature*, May 1963. Pound made minor charges in several of these cantos for *A Draft of XXX Cantos* (1930), especially alteration and condensation of Canto VI.

on tradition. It had to be based upon the present 'state of consciousness' as that state had been represented in literary form up
to the time when the modern poet began *in medias res*. In 1915 the
epic had seemed to stretch from Homer to Browning. Between 1915
and 1922, however, it became increasingly evident that the modern
consciousness had been discovered and expressed in prose. Therefore Pound had to come to terms with the prose tradition.

Ford Madox Ford had impressed on Pound as early as 1911 the
importance of 19th century prose, especially the style of Flaubert
(Mauberley's 'Penelope', if not Pound's own). But although Pound
at once sought in the theory and practice of imagism to incorporate
this 'prose' dimension, which meant for him 'realism' and which
enlarged the scope of poetry, his awareness of the range and uses of
prose techniques and subjects underwent continuing development
during his London years. Thus his first interest was Flaubert's
style, *le mot juste*, more than other aspects of Flaubert's art or his
overall literary achievement. A symptom of change appears as
early as 1914: Flaubert's 'varnish' seemed to lack the 'solidity' of
Stendhal's preoccupation with 'matter'. Pound's 1918 essays on
Henry James and Remy de Gourmont were less studies of style
than efforts to define in those writers a 'General summary of state
of human consciousness in decades immediately before my own';[3]
that is, to bring literary treatments of the western mind up to date.
He also discovered, however, that James and de Gourmont provided no answer to his own most pressing problem, the *form* in
which the modern consciousness might be treated. This frustration
is expressed in Canto VII, where he runs through a narrative tradition stretching from Homer, Ovid, the medieval epics, Dante,
Flaubert, and James to himself. As a guide 'drinking the tone' of
period atmospheres, James offers little help, nor, by itself, does the
Gourmontian apperceptivity of 'the live man'. Canto VII and the
original Canto VIII express nostalgia for the old epic subjects and
forms, but suggest no integration of the epic and prose traditions.

In 1922, however, Pound gained a new awareness of the prose
tradition as a development from the epic tradition. Pound had
moved to Paris. Having given a new direction to his life he was
seeking to give one to his poem. It was Flaubert's centennial year;
Pound read René Descharmes's recently published *Autour de
Bouvard et Pécuchet*. *Ulysses* appeared in book form. Pound, who
had followed it chapter by chapter since 1918, saw it as a whole for
the first time. Pound wrote several 'Paris Letters' for *The Dial* on

---

[3]'Date Line', 1934, *The Literary Essays of Ezra Pound* (1954).

Flaubert and Joyce. Of Flaubert he wrote: 'More and more we come to consider Flaubert as the great tragic writer, not the vaunted and perfect stylist. I mean that he is the tragedian of democracy, of modernity.[4] Both Flaubert and Joyce were 'classic' in that they represent 'everyman' even while writing *l'histoire morale contemporaine.* Flaubert had adumbrated a new modern form in *Bouvard*; Joyce had perfected that form in *Ulysses* and at the same time conflated the novel and the epic. In his 'Paris Letter' of May 1922 and in 'James Joyce et Pécuchet' Pound announced that every writer had to make a critique of *Ulysses* for his own use, 'afin d'avoir une idée nette du point d'arrivée de notre art, dans notre métier d'écrivain.'[5] These essays were his critique. They reflect a focusing of his thoughts about ways to handle the modern consciousness in contemporary yet classic form.

The results of this new view of Flaubert and Joyce can be seen in 'On Criticism In General' (*Criterion*, January 1923), a summary of 'The better tradition' Pound had been seeking to define throughout his London years. This history of literature — from Homer to Joyce, adapted to his own use — takes full account of an idea he had adumbrated in 1913 but only now stated categorically: that with Stendhal vital literary expression — at least work of epic scope — had 'gone over to prose'. Since Stendhal the main line had developed out of Flaubert, passed through the Goncourts, Dostoievsky, and James, and come to a final fruition in Joyce (Pound's table includes associates and followers of the previous writers, but Joyce stands alone). After Joyce, what? Pound appends enigmatically 'Fenollosa on the Chinese Ideograph'. By so doing he suggests that the next work is still to come. That he called this essay his *De Vulgari Eloquio* makes clear that it is his authoritative basis for *The Cantos*. His decision to begin his own poem as a modern *Odyssey*, in the wake of the prose *Ulysses* — 'an epochmaking report on the state of the human mind in the twentieth century (first of the new era),' i.e., testimony of 'the break' — was more than accidental.

Pound uses at the beginning of the *Pisan Cantos*, reflecting the beginning and progress of his entire poem, the phrase 'Odysseus the name of my family'. Joyce is also of that family, for Odysseus (Joyce called him 'Ulysses') evolved in Joyce's imagination and in

---

[4] *Dial*, September 1922, p. 333.

[5] 'James Joyce et Pécuchet' (written in French), *Mercure de France*, June 1, 1915; reprinted, *Polite Essays* (1937); an English translation, *Shenandoah*, Lexington, Va., Autumn, 1952. 'Paris Letter', *Dial*, June 1922; reprinted, *Literary Essays*, as 'Ulysses'.

his work just as it did in Pound's. Joyce wrote a schoolboy essay on Ulysses as his favourite hero. He considered calling *Dubliners* 'Ulysses in Dublin' and based a story on him, but, sensing that such a figure was too encyclopedic for a short story, put it aside. Having completed 'the moral history of my country' he went on to write his portrait of the artist who is seeking to free himself from the bonds of home, nation, and church so that he can 'forge in the smithy of my soul the uncreated conscience of my race'. Joyce's presentation of the typical modern city as a formative principle for the first time in English fiction, showing how its customs, institutions, and spiritual atmospheres paralyse its life, and his rendering of the conflict between this deadening milieu and the creative spirit, prepared the sequel. In *Ulysses* Joyce retained Stephen, the figure of his own alienation, intellectuality, creative impulse, and sense of history, but complemented him with the more comprehensive Bloom, *l'homme moyen sensuel* of 1904. He set them in a full presentation of the historical city, a material entity almost as alive as its denizens (conversely, the Dubliners appeared to be reduced to the city's materiality). He left them in the shadow of the historical city's biological counterpart, the non-intellectual force of physical nature, Molly Bloom. *Ulysses* is a personal epic in which the modern city-dwellers live their daily lives and enact their fates against a social, political, and metaphysical background that includes the history of western civilization at least since Homer.

Joyce develops a single idea toward an ever larger, more inclusive, synthetic form, until *Ulysses* becomes the culmination of the western epic tradition. Pound was in a perfect position to follow Joyce's progress, which is a precise parallel of his own. From 1914 on Pound corresponded with Joyce steadily, received his works chapter by chapter on their way to the magazines, and promoted his work in various reviews. Pound admired Joyce above all other contemporary writers; if he were a prose writer, he said, he would wish to write like Joyce. It was in one sense 'the Joyce decade'. In 1938 Pound recalled:

> In 1912 or eleven I invoked whatever gods may exist in the quatrain
>
>> Sweet Christ from hell spew up some Rabelais,
>> To belch and . . . and to define today
>> In fitting fashion, and her monument
>> Heap up to her in fadeless excrement.
>
> 'Ulysses' I take as my answer.[6]

---

[6]*Guide to Kulchur* (1938), p. 96.

Ulysses was the 'monumental' presentation of the modern consciousness; it registered comically the uncritical 'unification' of
19th-century thought which made modern man a thesaurus of inert ideas. 'Modernity', for Pound, was the as yet undiscovered relations among personality, the proliferating mechanism of the modern
city, and history. By expressing these relations *Ulysses* appeared
to end an era and clear the way for the new.

Pound used Joyce's books as whetstones while he himself was
seeking new artistic methods. In 1914 Joyce appeared as a prose
imagist who had invented a new form for short prose fiction; based
on the form of an emotion rather than the form of the short story,
it was perfectly adapted to register modern life both objectively
and as it struck the sensitive individual.[7] Joyce was able in *Dubliners* and *A Portrait* not merely to 'present' the urban surface, but
to make evident 'behind' his work his own 'sense of abundant
beauty', or personal vision. In his 1916 essay, ostensibly on *Exiles*,
Pound raises the whole problem of genres and modern realism and
decides that the novel, not the drama, is the form which the shaping intellect can use to encompass modern multiplicity. Yet Pound,
then in the midst of writing the early cantos and afflicted by the
problem of realism in poetry (he asks in old Canto I if he should
'sulk and leave the word to novelists?'), strains in his remarks on
the cinema, with *A Portrait* and his own work in mind, toward the
idea of a more concentrated, flexible form which might be built up
out of dramatic speech, melody, and the image. In 1918, having reread *A Portrait* and read the first chapters of *Ulysses*, he perceived
even more fully how Joyce's 'Swift alternation of subjective beauty
and external shabbiness, squalor, and sordidness' enabled him to
bring within his scope the most disparate matter of modern life,
from lyric and symbolic to naturalistic, and to achieve a maximum
concentration and historical depth. *Ulysses* appeared to be an even
further advance, for in Bloom Joyce had 'moved from autobiography to the creation of the complementary figure'. *Ulysses* was 'an
impassioned meditation on life', but the meditation was fictional-
ized: Bloom 'brings all life into the book. All Bloom is vital'. In 1922
Pound's enthusiasm increased. Boom appeared to encompass everything: he was a man immersed in modern life yet seen in the perspective of history; at the same time he expressed in his *monologue*

[7]The essays referred to in this paragraph are 'Dubliners and Mr. James
Joyce,' *Egoist*, 15 June 1914; 'The Non-Existence of Ireland', *New Age*, 25
February 1915; 'Mr. James Joyce and the Modern Stage', *Drama*, February
1916; and 'Joyce', *Future*, May 1918, augmented by 'Ulysses' for *Instigations*,
1920. The first and fourth appear in *Literary Essays*.

intérieur the integrity of the personal life and the vitality of a mind unconquered by the material world of things and forces. Bloom was a focus for what Pound was seeking in himself as man, as artist, and as the figure who spoke in his poems: he must reflect the novelist as receiver and recorder of *l'histoire morale contemporaine*, the historian who saw contemporaneity in the perspective of the past, and the lyrist who could express freely his desire and his ideal vision of the future.

In 'James Joyce et Pécuchet' Pound develops a synthetic view of Flaubert's career as the 19th century novelist-historian who had adumbrated a vision of the 20th. Flaubert had written works of contemporary realism in *Madame Bovary* and *L'Éducation Sentimentale*, and of historical exploration in *Salammbô* and *La Tentation de Saint Antoine*; he had sought to summarize these modes by historical juxtaposition in *Trois Contes*. But Pound's most absorbing new interest was the structure of *Bouvard et Pécuchet*. While *Madame Bovary* and *L'Éducation* record 19th-century provincial and city life in "une forme antérieure', *Bouvard* foreshadows the future by inaugurating a new form, the 'encyclopédie mise en farce'. *Bouvard* substitutes for the traditional form of the novel, with its naturalistic plot, an external form that reflects the structure of the mind, namely, *idées reçues* and the alphabet. The internal causality, *Bouvard et Pécuchet's* 'Défaut de methode dans les sciences' — motivating ideas but lack of a method to evaluate or use them effectively — appeared to be a crucial insight into modern mental reality. *Bouvard* gives the comic effect of men running in place while their surroundings stream past; there is an illusion of action, but it is really the stasis of a monument; despite the friends' purposefulness, their multiple interests, and their force, the mind is, as Pound put it, stuck in the mud, victimized by ideas which it receives passively rather than uses creatively. The book is an image of the mind as a single, paralyzed unification.

There was, however, another dimension to *Bouvard*. Flaubert was not merely presenting a *sottisier* and satirizing his characters; he was conducting what Pound called in his essay on *Exiles* 'a combat with the phantoms of the mind'. Flaubert used his own researches, in which he had discovered the encyclopedia to be the form of the mind of his time. He turned his researches into literature within that form, which both renders the mind and motivates it. Thus he fictionalizes his own struggle in his characters. The encyclopedia is his 'setting' or world, and his characters, like himself, are its victims. But Flaubert also stands outside of the fiction as the stylist, the

heroic artist who exercises his act of art and whose energy gives the
book life. The character is a mask, but the style is the man. In this
sense Flaubert is opposing the creative personality to its environ-
ment: within it he is a victim; as the narrator he is the lyrist, or
perhaps even would-be epist, a potential Odysseus whose motive is
to renew the world.

Joyce's brilliant innovation in *Ulysses* synthesized Flaubert's
work and his own; it also added to 'the international store of literary technique'. Pound lauded Joyce's form unreservedly. Instead of
writing historical novels and realistic novels or using the static
structure of the encyclopedia, Joyce had integrated within his
Homeric 'scaffold' the chaotic multiplicity of modern life, an archetypal hero, a compelling plot, and a vertical depth which evokes
history and myth: 'Joyce combine le moyen âge, les ères classiques,
même l'antiquité juive, dans une action actuelle.' By comparison,
Flaubert 'échelonne les époques', and *Bouvard* is inferior in architecture and narrative drive. Within the objective form of the scaffold Joyce could make autobiography, in the persons of Stephen
and Bloom, his subject matter. Stephen, who has an historian's
mind, is a victim of history, and Bloom, 'a receiver of all things' who
has a novelist's, is a victim of his surroundings. Yet in their *monologues intérieurs* they express the freedom of the mind and the emotions. Their 'tones of mind' are personal on one side, yet on the
other 'realist', for they correspond to modern realities. These 'tones
of mind' provide the basis for the narrator's overview of his action.
For Pound the vitality of *Ulysses* rose from Joyce's presenting his
'tones of mind' in a 'many-tongued and multiple language'. As the
controlling mind and synthesizing stylist who imposes on Ulysses
its varied forms and methods, Joyce includes the entire fiction in his
encompassing voice, a version of the epic voice. Thus his vision of
the modern world, and of the modern consciousness in the perspective of history, emerges as a personal construction which yet derives
full validation from its modern surface, its naturalistic characterization and plot, and its historical scaffold. Joyce's intellectual vitality
and intensity unite novelist, historian, and lyrist; in so far as the
proportion of balance are perfect, and imply or are suspended in a
comprehensive philosophy of life, these three make Joyce a (modern) epic writer. Joyce succeeds Flaubert as the ultimate Odyssean,
having at last made the figure of himself both the centre and the
encompasser of his fiction.

But although Joyce had freed the idealizing sensibility from total
subjection to the present, Bloom remained a receiver of all things,

Stephen remained detached from the outer world, and *Ulysses* looked toward the past. For Pound the difference between the passive hero and an active one was the difference between prose analysis and poetic synthesis. In the face of the prose tradition Pound had been trying sporadically since 1912 to define the possibilities and limits of poetry. In 1918, faced with Henry James's representation of *moeurs contemporaines*, which remained embedded in period costume and feeling, he attempted a theoretical definition:

'Most good prose arises, perhaps, from an instinct of negation; is the detailed, convincing analysis of something detestable; of something which one wants to eliminate. Poetry is the assertion of a positive, i.e. of desire, and endures for a longer period. Poetic satire is only an assertion of this positive, inversely, i.e. as of an opposite hatred. . . . Poetry = Emotional synthesis, quite as real, quite as realist as any prose (or intellectual) analysis. . . . This is a highly untechnical, unimpressionist, in fact almost theological manner of statement, but is perhaps the root difference between the two arts of literature.'[8]

For Pound the prose tradition had discovered the conditions of modern consciousness; poetry had to accept those conditions but go beyond them. 'Emotional synthesis' required the apperceptivity of an urbane, historically aware sensibility like that of de Gourmont, an 'artist of the nude' or 'permanent human elements' (like Pound's Propertius, or his Acoetes of Canto II). Only out of emotional awareness could a new consciousness (a new ethic and a new city) be built ('We base our "science" on perceptions, but our ethics have not yet attained this palpable basis'). Such a new ethic or 'city' began and ended with the personal: 'Civilization is individual. The truth is the individual'.[9] But any 'assertion of a positive' required volition as well as apperceptivity; poetry demands 'some sort of vigour, some sort of assertion, some sort of courage, or at least of ebullience that throws a certain amount of remembered beauty into an unconquered consciousness'.[10] Joyce's city was a bankrupt paralytic unification of which Joyce remained a 'receiver'; to revitalize urbanity or community the mind would have first to break down inert orders, then rediscover living fragments of thought and feeling from the matter of past and present, and finally reshape these by the creative effort of the poetic mind. By such notions Pound had

---

[8]'Henry James', *Literary Essays*, p. 324.

[9]'Remy de Gourmont', *Literary Essays*, pp. 340, 345, 355.

[10]Pound is thinking of d'Annunzio versus Proust, *Dial*, November 1922, p. 554.

been working toward a method of giving form to his concept of the heroic artist as a troubadour in the root sense: a 'maker and finder of songs' (the phrase comes from Whitman), whose 'making' would receive objective validation from his 'finding' of his matter and his forms in history and nature.

Pound defined epic from the personal standpoint as 'the speech of a nation through the mouth of one man' (1909), and from the objective standpoint as 'a poem including history' (1933). These definitions imply that the 'one man', the lyrist and in Pound's sense the hero himself, must be objectified, that is, identified with the nation or speech or 'world' which he took as his subject. Pound had assumed from the start the classic 'vocational' conception of the epic poet: that he was a synthetic or 'donative' artist who built upon his predecessors and whose work was a continuation of theirs, and that his own career was not merely a personal one, but itself a part of history. One of the things he was doing with Flaubert's and Joyce's careers was to give them a shape, especially Joyce's. Thus he saw Joyce as a figure who had worked through the lyric mode of *Chamber Music* to the novelistic mode of *Dubliners*; had then integrated the novelistic and lyric modes in *A Portrait*; had experimented with the objectivity of drama in *Exiles*; and had concluded this development in the epic synthesis of *Ulysses*. He also found parallels between *Dubliners* and *Trois Contes, A Portrait* and *L'Éducation, Ulysses* and *Bouvard*. In short, not only did Joyce epitomize in his work the modern artist's formation of an objective literary tradition, but his personal career was itself a pattern validated both by tradition and by a struggle which had turned that career into a classic monument.

Pound had been schematizing his own career during the fallow years 1920–1921 while he was reassessing his American and London past to seek a new direction (such reassessment is a personal version of the *nostos*).[11] In 'Main outline of E. P.'s work to date' (*Umbra*, 1920) he reflected the historical, novelistic, and personal strains. The 'Personae' of 1908–1911, his early dramatic lyrics, were objective expressions of past emotions in forms adapted from Browning, Yeats, and the 1890s. The 'Sketches' of *Ripostes* and *Lustra* had thrown the emphasis toward *moeurs contemporaines*, using the

---

[11]It should also be noted that Pound had written in 1917-18 'Studies in Contemporary Mentality' (*New Age*), a survey of British magazines which he called in 'Date Line' his Flaubertian *sottisier*. All of Pound's prose collections are intended to 'have a design', and in that sense are efforts to give form to his public career as his poetry gives form to his poetic career.

avant garde techniques Pound had denominated as imagism. The
three 'Major Personae' —'The Seafarer', 'The Exile's Letter (and
Cathay in general)', and *Homage to Sextus Propertius* — were efforts to define figures who would objectify, and place in a better or
larger tradition than either the British or American traditions then
available to a poet writing in English, his personal motives. *Propertius* (1918) was Pound's first successful large form to integrate the
motives of lyrist, novelist, and historian. Previously he had written
many 'series', all of which he subsequently broke down into single
poems because they failed to achieve any unity except the unity of
the single personality behind them (e.g., a collection of early personae intended as 'a more or less proportional presentation of life';
'Und Drang' (*Canzoni*, 1911); and 'groups' of poems in *Lustra*). He
had tried historical juxtaposition of the amatory customs of two
cultures in *Homage à la Langue d'Oc*, a sequence of Provençal
adaptations Gourmontian in their expression of emotion, and
Moeurs Contemporaines, Jamesian sketches of London (1917).

In *Propertius* Pound used the 'major persona' to give full expression to the state of civilization in London. *Propertius* is, however,
the poem of a poet who, although opposing the prevailing civilization, speaks from within it. Even as he concluded *Propertius* his
motive was expanding, leading him away from London toward a
search for the new, as *Mauberley* and Canto VII make evident. In
Mauberley, which he called (misleadingly) a version of *Propertius*
with a modernist surface, he tried to summarize his life in London
by placing it against the background of both the prose tradition (it
('condenses a James novel') and the epic tradition (including, one
should not forget, Whitman). Mauberley, a figure like Frederick
Moreau or Stephen Dedalus, reflects the modern artist in historical
and Odyssean perspectives. Just as Joyce had multiplied himself in
Stephen, Bloom, and the voice of his narrator to enlarge his form
and thereby encompass a more complex reality, Pound divided the
objectified passive figure Mauberley, artist-hero manqué, from the
active narrator whose voice dominates the poem. But although
Mauberley seeks to use an objectified figure, at least nominally, it
is still a 'study in form'; Pound is exploring the relation between
the traditions of poetry and prose rather than having successfully
fused them. Actually *Mauberley*, like Canto VII, records 'the break'
— in all aspects of culture and in his own life — of which Pound
became aware following World War I.

In *Poems 1918–21* Pound tried to suggest an even larger summary of his work, in Flaubertian fashion, by juxtaposing *Proper-

tius, Langue d'Oc/Moeurs Contemporaines, and *Mauberley* as *Three Portraits* of, respectively, Rome, Provence-London, and London. As in *Trois Contes* these historical tableaux all revolved around a theme line — for Pound's triptych, Propertius's 'My genius is no more than a girl'; in the sense that the portraits also constitute representations of London, he also seems to have been seeking on a larger scale than in *Propertius* alone the kind of vertical historical depth which Joyce was achieving in *Ulysses*. All of these reassessments and reorderings, however, reflect the misgivings about epic form Pound had expressed when he asked if he should 'sulk and leave the word to novelists?' His exasperation about the state of western civilization and his efforts to extend his conception of history to social, economic, and political dimensions were having effects on his poetry: partly growing pains, but partly also personal discouragement. He frequently (most often to Joyce) deplored the *passéism* of his subjects and forms; he repeated this misgiving in 1922 in congratulating Eliot on *The Waste Land*. As already noted, from 1919 to 1922 he was at an impasse about the increasing formlessness and obscurity of his poem. It is against this background that we should see his reactions to Flaubert and Joyce in 1922 and his reorganizing of his poem sometime in 1923.

In his 1909 letter to his mother Pound wrote that an epic writer needed 'a beautiful tradition', 'a unity in the outline of that tradition', 'a hero, mythical or historical', and the equivalent of divine machinery. He had begun his poem without either the outline or the hero, seeking to follow the method Dante had used to escape from such epic requirements ('he dips into a multitude of traditions and unifies them by their connection with himself'). Joyce's crucial innovation, his Homeric scaffold, gave the prose and epic traditions the unity of outline Pound is seeking in Canto VII and finds in his 1922 essays. Pound's first canto represents, as well as the tragedy of 'Europe exhausted by the conquest of Alsace-Lorraine', which can be called the theme of Cantos I–XVI, a tiered historical depth in its conflation of Homer, the Anglo-Saxon 'The Seafarer', and Divus's Renaissance Latin version of the *Odyssey*, in the language and voice of the 20th century American. But more important it throws his poem forward with a compelling fiction: a story of action, an archetypal hero, and the idea of the *nostos*. By starting with the voyage to the land of the dead Pound made the *nostos* symbolize a theory of history. It is the archetype for 'the break' and for his motive of exploring the past in order to find the basis for a return journey which will itself be the process of building a new civilization; according to the Homeric parallel the *nostos* would be completed when the poet, in the wake of Odysseus, became united again with Penelope (the archetypal woman, for Pound a symbol of beauty): their union would symbolize a reconstituted Ithaca (the city of the imagination, Pound's 'city of Dioce'). The *nostos* is also a figure for a journey of the mind; as Pound wrote to Williams in 1908, 'the soul, from god, returns to him. But anyone who can trace that course or symbolize it by anything not wandering. . . .' In this visionary or Neoplatonic sense the *nostos* is the search for what Pound called a 'philosophy', a metaphysic which would validate an ethic, a morality, and a politics. Both the fiction and the philosophy are based, however, on personal experience. In the 'periplum', or voyage on which experience is encountered directly, the hero sees many cities and manners of men and knows their minds. He also enters the world of myth and encounters divinities. Both kinds of encounter also become the occasion for personal insights, the aesthetic perceptions ('gods,' or states of mind) which form the basis of Pound's visions of a permanent world of truth.

Pound modifies Joyce's use of the *Odyssey* by making his scaffold merely imply form rather than impose a fixed progression. For, Pound's form had to be open: he was seeking to build up the new from the very bottom out of modern experience (Pound's method should be carefully differentiated from the 'mythical method' as Eliot defined it from Joyce and used it: 'manipulating a continuous parallel between contemporaneity and antiquity').[12] Thus whereas Joyce's scaffold adheres closely to Homer, Pound's is a universal archetype of epic form, an overarching ideal structure which the modern poet must in one sense fill and in another sense make new. Pound was careful even in designating the scaffold of *Ulysses* 'un moyen de régler la forme' to emphasize the stylist's conception and the work he built up within it:

'These correspondences are part of Joyce's mediaevalism and are chiefly his own affair, a scaffold, a means of construction, justified by the result, and justifiable by it only. The result is a triumph in form, in balance, a main schema, with continuous inweaving and arabesque.'[13]

In the most limited sense Pound's personae had been scaffolds, but they represented only isolated moments; the shaky division between mask and poet in *Mauberley* is symptomatic of Pound's need to separate the poet from the mask so that he can enlarge his scope.

---

[12]' "Ulysses," Order, and Myth', *Dial*, November 1923.

[13]'Paris Letter', *Literary Essays*, p. 406.

In the broadest sense the scaffold is the entire literary tradition, and in that sense a pattern of the human mind itself (one can see in the rejected early versions of Pound's poem the failure of an effort to use 'the tradition' or 'the mind of Europe' — and America — merely as an ideal concept hazily defined by the external, arbitrary scaffold of the Dantean or Whitmanian canto). The scaffold as Pound finally conceived and used it can be thought of as a potential 'overplot', while the direct experience can be thought of as welling up from a kind of 'underplot'. These two meet on the surface of *The Cantos* in the activity of the poet; the motive of *The Cantos* is toward their perfect integration.

Formally speaking, the point of Canto I is its momentary synthesis of epic form and the poet's own modern experience. Canto II, denying the Browning method of using history directly, without myth, introduces Pound's basic mode of sensibility, the 'magic moment' of insight into a permanent world constituted of the human figure, the elements, and the state of mind as a 'god'; his humanistic version of Christianity's revelation, conception, and incarnation. After these *trouvailles* (which imply the whole poem as do the exordium and invocation of the classical epic, though as 'prophecies'), Canto III returns to the present to express, as still part of the fiction, the failure of old Cantos I–III because of a lack of a scaffold: in doing so Canto III presents Pound's own meditations on a failed voyage, a failed 'magic moment', and a failed *nostos*; it ends in mere desolation. Cantos IV–VII, still rehearse as intermittent vision Pound's struggle of 1915–19 to accommodate the muse of epic, Calliope, who is providing the forms which arise in the modern poet's mind, and Truth, the muse of fact, who supplies unformed historical data, whether they be fragments from the past previously unformed or the modern poet's own life. The conflict, which emerges explicitly in the exordium to the Malatesta Cantos (VIII–XI), is resolved in those cantos as the modern poet speaks in many voices — narrator, chronicler of the times, retrospective historian, and Sigismundo's compatriot, among others — to bring Sigismundo's ethos to life in an epic frame. Thus, whereas the 'ply over ply' of 'tiered' history in Canto I was a poetic *trouvaille*, here the poet builds it up methodically out of unformed matter.[14] With the assurance gained the poet 'sees' modern 'facts' within the

[14]Myles Slatin (op. cit.) hypothesizes that Pound discovered his form and motive from his work on the Malatesta Cantos, spontaneously, as in an action painting. This is the side of the 'underplot', or 'fact'. But Pound had to have a coherent theory of history and literary history, defined as a potential 'overplot', as well as confidence in the spontaneous creative act.

Homeric frame (Canto XII).[15] Able now both to *enter* past forms
and to *use* them, he sustains in Cantos XIV–XVI a neo-Dantean
dream narrative during which he encounters the modern 'dead' as
infernal states of mind, as anecdotes about the war, and as radio
voices, all of which signify the fading away of western civilization as
a viable culture. It is with Canto XVII, which picks up the interrupted 'So that' from the end of Canto I (he is now *with* the dead,
all history now being one), that the Odyssean scaffold is fully actuated. Canto XVII introduces a coherent fictional venture, by the
modern poet in his own person, into original myth, a mystical-
artistic state of mind; though fleeting, it is a testimony that the
effort to give form to experience is on the right track.

Within the Odyssean frame, then, Pound's overriding narrative
voice, which often comes to the surface as the modern poet speaks
in his own person, expresses the process of the mind as it moves
through all eras seeking materials and capturing them in the myr-
iad forms the mind uses to reify and communicate its discoveries.
These forms are appropriated by a narrator who, as Pound had been
in London, is city-saturated, historically and contemporaneously.
The potential form of the archetypal scaffold and an encyclopæ-
dic principle which might be called 'the unlimitedness of forms'
(Pound's polytheistic states of mind), make it theoretically possible
to include any kind of experience. Like Flaubert and Joyce, Pound
draws on all the arts (e.g., literature, history, journalism, philology,
economics, theology, physics, music, politics) and all the techniques
(e.g., narrative, monologue, anecdote, litany), thus solving Bouvard
and Pécuchet's and even Bloom's 'Défaut de methode dans les
sciences'. He assumes that the permanent forms of nature and the
permanent forms of the human mind, which are reflected in whatever men have made (or will make), undergo perpetual metamorphosis (changes of phase, emergence and recession, perfection
and decay, etc.); to renew these forms, to create new syntheses out
of permanent materials, and even to invent, expresses not simple
recurrences of cycles, but continuous creative renovation. The
energizing principle of Pound's poem is not Flaubert's objective
narrative voice nor the voice of Joyce's unseen stylist. Rather the

---

[15]Canto XIII, Confucius, is a new 'potential' element, 'seen' because the poet
can sustain vision; it does not become actuated until later in the poem. Canto
XIII is Pound's version of Whitman's 'Passage to India'; it extends the scope
of *The Cantos* toward its true epic subject, the idea and vision of 'one world'
that had begun to emerge as a fact in 1914. Pound has tried to 'forge in the
smithy of his soul the uncreated conscience of one world'.

spoken voice of urbane conversation tries to reflect at once the creative process of aesthetic perception, free will, and intellectual shaping; the objective nature of its materials; and the moment in which conversation creates an audience whose view of reality is subject to change like the speaker's. The past, the past as it is brought to life in the present, and the present itself, as mental and emotional experience, are being discovered, absorbed, interpreted, and applied to create the future.

To what extent Pound's *Cantos* is wholly successful is still unclear. It may not be possible for one man, however intelligent, perceptive, and purposeful (and many of Pound's ideas are certainly questionable), to induce from the fragments of civilization a new literary and cultural synthesis. There is no question, however, that he composed and reshaped *A Draft of XVI Cantos* with great care, not only introducing the *Odyssey* scaffold but interpolating elsewhere direct and indirect indications of its primacy. When we learn to read *The Cantos* more thoroughly in the light of traditional epic conventions; to assess exactly the carefully modulated relation of the contemporary speaker to his facts and forms; to interpret indicated connections between cantos; and to see modern poetic techniques in their proper perspective: then, I think, we shall see that Pound has achieved within his scaffold a more distinct progression — line by line, passage by passage, canto by canto — than has been so far discovered. But whatever the final judgment, it is precisely the effort 'to build the city of Dioce, whose terraces are the colour of stars', which makes Pound, like Joyce, one of the great witnesses to the artist's effort to encompass the 20th century. Though Pound's Europe, his structure of ideas, and perhaps his poem seemed to collapse, the dream remained 'in the heart indestructible', for, in the Pisan stockade, the voice continued. There is no mistaking that at Pisa a meeting takes place between the Odyssean poet and some goddess, confirming our feeling that a dispersed personality has reconstituted itself out of bits of its past, out of the wreckage of Europe, out of his Pisan surroundings, and out of earned permanent truths. If *Bouvard et Pécuchet* is a monument to the Second Empire and *Ulysses* a monument to Europe on the verge of World War I, *The Cantos* may be a monument to the tragic failure of many visions held between the two wars. Joyce and Pound are both Flaubert's successors in an Odyssean tradition. Even more directly than Flaubert, attempting to resolve the post-romantic division between history and the self, they used their own lives as their subject matter and tried to make personality and history the two bases from which the present might pass into the future, giving new life to the achievements which make civilization a great expression of man.

Herbert N. Schneidau

Tradition, Myth, and Imagist Poetics

Many literary comparisons have been proposed for *The Cantos*: Homer and Dante obviously, lately and suggestively *Piers Plowman,* and perhaps we should add Blake's Prophetic Books. But the best analogy of all is surely Ovid's *Metamorphoses,* a work that Pound seems unable to praise too much. Ovid, however, was not "writing" mythology, but rather constructing a living compendium of myth, gathering together metamorphic interpretations of realities. So also with Pound, who retells certain vital segments of myth, flashes of man's intercourse with the "vital universe," rendering them in his own "interpretative metaphors." Like Fenollosa he believes in language carrying alluvial deposits of these meanings, hence his interest in the layers of language, e.g., in various translations of Homer. Those layers preserve live speech, on the importance of which Hueffer, Fenollosa, and Frobenius agree. Its importance is not diminished by literacy or the advance of culture: "The spoken idiom is not only a prime factor, but certainly one of the most potent, progressively so as any modality of civilization ages."[1] In the later Cantos Pound makes use of the term "Sagetrieb, or the oral tradition," and plainly means it to apply to his poem: "There is no mystery about the Cantos, they are the tale of the tribe — give Rudyard credit for his use of the phrase."[2] Trying

Reprinted from *Ezra Pound: The Image and the Real* (Baton Rouge: Louisiana State University Press, 1969), pp. 136-46, by permission of the author and the publisher.

[1] "Date Line," first printed in *Make it New* (1934); see *Literary Essays,* 77.
[2] Canto LXXXIX; *Guide to Kulchur,* 194.

to convince prospective readers that the poem was not a *tour de force* of polyglot scholia, he stated: "There *is* at start, descent to the shades, metamorphoses, parallel (Vidal-Actaeon). All of which is mere matter for little . . . rs and Harvud instructors *unless* I pull it off as reading matter, singing matter, shouting matter, the tale of the tribe."[3] Though he did not care for Mallarmé, he has plainly attempted to give a more pure sense to the words of the tribe, filing with his Imagist precision the tropes and images that serve as his Luminous Details, but always remembering the oral source.

With his "Sagetrieb" Pound was trying to overcome a serious handicap in the way of modern understanding of mythology; this is the ingrained assumption that creation must be "original" and "individual," that the author cannot make use of his material in its primitive form but must make it conform to his personal pattern. But a "cult of personality" violates the whole spirit of mythology, which is communal or cultic rather than individual. The high-water mark of the age of myth, in Pound's eyes, was the institution of the Eleusinian mysteries, which provided integration into a community (although it did not, like less moderate mysticisms, allow the individual to sink into an "unconditioned ground of being"). For Pound "our time has overshadowed the mysteries by an over-emphasis on the individual. . . . Eleusis did not distort truth by exaggerating the individual, neither could it have violated the individual spirit."[4] The extension of the view of myth as communal is that "literature rises in racial process" and should express what Frobenius called *Kulturmorphologie* rather than individual "creativity." So Pound in aiming at the "tale of the tribe" was bound to leave himself open to the suspicion that he lacked originality; it was a risk he was prepared to run in order to get the "spoken tradition" onto paper.

Pound believed that his poem was being written at that point in history when it was possible to extricate myth from the pigeonhole of "fable and allegory" at last, thanks to the insights of men like Frobenius who saw in it a "reality" beyond the usual definitions of that term. In one of the passages in *Guide to Kulchur* asserting that "the gods exist," he remarks that "it has taken two thousand years

[3]*Letters*, 294.

[4]*Guide to Kulchur*, 299. A true work of communal myth is of course "poetry of reality"; cf. Canto XCIX: "This is not a work of fiction/nor yet of one man." Also note his remark in "Prolegomena": "It is tremendously important that great poetry be written, it makes no jot of difference who writes it" (*Literary Essays*, p. 10).

to get round again to meditating on mythology."[5] Yet the implication is present in Pound's arguments that the knowledge has been
in the air all along, borne on the stream of tradition. Gemisthus
Plethon and John Heydon, among others, knew what we know. For-
tunately for Pound's purpose, the Christian Neo-Platonics were
in the habit of taking pagan myth seriously, as one more set of
hieroglyphics by which God revealed truth to the world.[6] So he
found many precedents for such statements as "I assert that a great
treasure of verity exists for mankind in Ovid."

Ovid's great work provides yet another major analogue to the art
of *The Cantos* in its organization. Pound never assumed that unity
was Ovid's aim, but rather took the *Metamorphoses* to be a compendium of its varied sources and insights, multi-layered and multi-
faceted. Pound was alert to the signs of various strata preserved in
the great traditional works; in the *Odyssey* he saw the journey to
Hades as the primal layer: "The Nekuia shouts aloud that it is
older than the rest, all that island, Cretan, etc., hinter-time."[7]
Following this line of thought he concluded that the whole idea of
unity had been distorted: "I suspect neither Homer nor Dante *had*
the kind of boring 'unity' of surface that we take to be characteristic of Pope, Racine, Corneille."[8] He even began to suspect that
Homer's apparent unity might be the result of tampering by editors,
and reinforced his suspicion by musing on works of tradition whose
permanence is certainly not due to any " 'unity' of surface":

> Pisistratus found the Homeric texts in disorder, we don't quite know
> what he did about it. The Bible is a compendium, people trimmed it
> to make it solid. It has gone on for ages, because it wasn't allowed to
> overrun all the available parchment . . . . Ovid's Metamorphoses are
> a compendium, not an epic like Homer's; Chaucer's Canterbury
> Tales are a compendium of all the good yarns Chaucer knew. The
> Tales have lasted through centuries while the long-winded medieval
> narratives went into museums.[9]

It should be pointed out that these remarks are the substance
of the page of the *ABC of Reading* devoted to the "DICHTEN =
CONDENSARE" principle. Pound apparently believes that if a

---

[5]*Guide to Kulchur*, 125.
[6]Gombrich, "*Icones Symbolicae*," 169.
[7]*Letters*, 274.
[8]*Ibid.*
[9]*ABC of Reading*, 92.

poet really concentrates his work, the logical result is a compendium; a long unified tale can be produced only by spreading the
effort. He assumes that the immortality of his illustrative works is
due to such concentration. The list of examples might be extended,
with the Confucian Odes for instance; the applicability to *The
Cantos* is obvious.

If a poet proposes to himself to write not a "myth for our time"
but a huge process-epic carrying the burden of a "tradition" embodied in various layers of language and racial consciousness, how
could his work be anything other than a compendium? Various
phrases are now coming into use to suggest the new conventions
that Pound and other modernists have utilized: composition by
field, diffusion as organization, and others. But for Pound's work
the root of the matter is that real concentration boils a work down
to separate "gists and piths," which must seem at first fragmentary
and disunified. He has never desired a unity of surface or style, nor
made a secret of the "binding matter" in *The Cantos* which, while
holding the poem together, has made it seem even more hetero-
geneous. This matter includes, for instance, annotations: "Part of
the job is *finally* to get all the necessary notes into the text itself.
Not only are the LI Cantos a part of the poem, but by labeling most
of 'em draft, I retain right to include *necessary* explanations in
LI-C or in revision." He added in explanation of this procedure that
"Binyon has shown that Dante needs *fewer* notes than are usually
given the student," the implication being that Dante too worked
his notes into the text.[10] Insofar as Pound really hoped to write
"the tale of the tribe" his work must be endless, episodic, and con-
glomerate, justifying itself only in the sharp etching of those bits
of fact that "govern knowledge as the switchboard governs an
electric circuit." The very precision demanded in the etching of
those details prevents them from being subordinated to any unifying principle; tonal or thematic unity imposed by a single mind, no
matter how creative, tends to diminish the sense of jagged clarity.
If the texture is made smooth, the details cannot stand out sharply.
As we have seen, Pound suspects that there has been some homoge-
nizing of Homer's surface, so that only now are we beginning to
notice just how clearly and accurately his details preserve the
knowledge of his time. The ancient Greeks must have seen more
than "a good story" in Homer, to make him the basis of their
educational system.

----

[10]*Letters*, 293.

Thus, though *The Cantos* have plenty of "themes" and "links,"
everything is not subordinated to them, and Pound never seeks the
kind of imposed external form that would make his work seem more
readily graspable. A clear idea of his values and predilections in
this area can be found in his defense of the work of William Carlos
Williams, another believer in living language:

> Very well, he does not "conclude"; his work has been "often form-
> less," "incoherent," opaque, obscure, obfuscated, confused, trun-
> cated, etc. . . . But it can do us no harm to stop an hour or so and
> consider the number of very important chunks of world-literature in
> which form, major form, is remarkable mainly for absence [such as
> the *Iliad*, Aeschylus' *Prometheus*, Montaigne, Rabelais, *Bouvard
> and Pécuchet*].
>
> The component of these great works and *the* indispensable com-
> ponent is texture; which Dr. Williams indubitably has in the best,
> and in increasingly frequent, passages of his writing.[11]

The Cantos too seek texture rather than major form. In this case
Pound was arguing not merely from a technical point of view, but
from a religious or metaphysical one, from a belief that the polytheistic, metamorphic character of oral and epic tradition necessi-
tates "formlessness." He remarks in paragraphs that immediately
precede the defense of Williams' work:

> We are still so generally obsessed by monism and monotheistical
> backwash, and ideas of orthodoxy that we (and the benighted Brit-
> ons) can hardly observe a dissociation of ideas without thinking a
> censure is somehow therein implied . . . . as if monism or monothe-
> ism were anything more than a hypothesis agreeable to certain
> types of very lazy minds too weak to bear an uncertainty or to re-
> main in "uncertainty."

The use of Keats's "negative capability" principle can only have
been meant to imply that the same weakness that chooses mono-
theism to assuage its uncertainties is also responsible for the over-
emphasis on tidy and symmetrical forms. Williams, for Pound a
salient example of "racial process" in literature, is credited with
"Mediterranean equipment," which puts him in the line with the
other great "Mediterranean" artists, from Homer to Flaubert, who
have created "formless" works; Pound clearly believes that the

---

[11]"Dr. Williams' Position, *Dial*, LXXXV (November 1928); *Literary Essays*,
394-95.

natural polytheism of Mediterranean myth is racially ingrained
in these artists, and that it accounts for their heterogeneity. In
Pound's thinking on myth the stress is always on "many gods,"
diversities of insight, and varieties of presentation. Very possibly his
adverse reaction to Milton's imposition of Latinate form on his material was part of a deeper reaction against what he would feel to be
a restricted religious insight.

When asked anxious questions about the form of *The Cantos*,
Pound's replies usually tried to indicate that the poem was not
schematic, but organic in the most literal sense — growing: "As to
the *form* of *The Cantos*: All I can say or pray is: *wait* till it's there.
I mean wait till I get 'em written and then if it don't show, I will
start exegesis. I haven't an Aquinas-map; Aquinas *not* valid now."[12]
Some critics have read this to mean that somehow, at the end, out
of a hat, Pound was going to try to come up with a principle that
would run backwards and make order where there was only chaos
before. Such critics tend to sit back with an air of triumph as the
poem grows. But since the whole idea of imposed form goes against
everything Pound has stood for, I suggest we take literally his advice not to look for the hidden Aquinas-map. What he did expect,
probably, was that the *Sagetrieb* would show more clearly at the
end. This is not to say that *The Cantos* are an aleatoric "action
painting," of course. Pound has never been willing to discard the
values of intelligence and consciousness: he likened creative effort
without intellectual control to a railway engine without tracks.[13]
It is not likely that his habits of composition were so literally scat-
terbrained as the "action painting" analogy implies; and in his Vorticist writings he derided "automatism."

Study of Pound's writings has convinced me that even by the
most hostile evaluation his mind was never so disorganized as to
prevent him from imposing "form" on *The Cantos* if he had wanted
to. It rather seems that his principles of composition were governed
by two great values he derived from "the tradition" — medieval
exact distinctions and Ovidian multiplicity. It can even be dem-
onstrated that these two poles of his tradition had for him a
connection:

> I cannot repeat too often that there was a profound psychological
> knowledge in medieval Provence, however Gothic its expression;
> that men, concentrated on certain validities, attaining an exact and

---

[12]*Letters*, 323.
[13]*Literary Essays*, 71.

diversified terminology, have there displayed considerable penetration; that this was carried into early Italian poetry; and faded from
it when metaphors became decorative instead of interpretative; and
that the age of Aquinas would not have tolerated sloppy expression
of psychology concurrent with the exact expression of "mysticism."
There is also great wisdom in Ovid.[14]

The connection of course is in the belief that precise and vital language and detail, as in Cavalcanti, Ovid, or the "spoken tradition"
generally, can preserve knowledge even of a highly esoteric order.
    That tradition-derived values such as precision, "Luminous De-
tail," and the like accord with Imagist principles will, I hope, readily be granted. But there is an even deeper relationship between
Imagist ideas and those which find their first articulation in "Psychology and Troubadours," having to do with the use of visions. We
are now coming to recognize that large parts of *The Cantos* are
records of visionary activity. Robert Fitzgerald recorded on a visit
to Rapallo that Pound dropped the remark " 'I live in music for
days at a time.' He did not mean the wordless music of the com-
posers — Vivaldi, Antheil — who then interested him, but the music within himself, a visionary music requiring words. I knew that
this applied to *The Cantos*."[15] I believe that Fitzgerald was right to
interpret "music" in this way. This might explain a remark Pound
made to Margaret Anderson in 1918: "Chère amie, I am, for the
time being, bored to death with being any kind of an editor. I desire
to go on with my long poem; and like the Duke of Chang, I desire to
hear the music of a lost dynasty. (Have managed to hear it, in
fact.)"[16] On the referential level, "music" here might refer to the
Provençal sound-values which he was trying to resurrect, but since
he always connected that aspect of Troubadour poetry with their
penetration of certain secrets of the universe, I am satisfied that the
term has a larger sense here, and that the "music" of *The Cantos*
has a mystical substratum. Any "visions" Pound may have culti-
vated would have had words and music as well as visual registration.
The connection with Imagism comes in the fact that at least once
Pound defined Imagism so as to lay a heavy emphasis on its vision-

---

[14]*Ibid.*, 344. (From the essay on Remy de Gourmont of 1920.)

[15]Quoted by Norman, *Ezra Pound*, 310.

[16]*Letters*, 128. At least one of Pound's statements implies that he had been ex-
periencing visions since 1910 or earlier: "No man who has not passed through,
or nearly approached that spiritual experience known as illumination — I use
the word in a technical sense — can appreciate the *Paradiso* to the full" (*The
Spirit of Romance*, 144).

ary potential: he called it "poetry wherein the feelings of painting and sculpture are predominant (certain men move in phantasmagoria; the images of their gods, whole countrysides, stretches of hill and forest, travel with them)."[17] "Phantasmagoria" is presumably that which is produced by the activity of the *phantastikon*, which Pound had been cultivating since 1912.

Pound made the above definition in 1920, very likely as a result of pondering how his Imagist purposes fitted the program for his long poem. But it suggests a perspective for looking back at all Pound's work since 1912, the year that produced both Imagism and "Psychology and Troubadours." This perspective is useful in spite of the fact that Pound did undergo a reaction against the "mushiness" of some mystical thought. I have described elsewhere in some detail the growth of Pound's boredom with Yeats's "psychical research" and his loss of patience with some muzzy forms of Orientalism; but I would add to that account a note that the same letter that makes a derogatory remark about Yeats's spiritualism also contains a recommendation of Upward's *Divine Mystery* and *New Word*.[18] Rejecting the looser mysticism, he cleaved to more "exact" kinds. And there is one final detail that helps reconcile any seeming disparities in his thought on these subjects. In his obituary article on Hueffer, Pound made a striking revelation: "That Ford was almost an *halluciné* few of his intimates can doubt. He felt until it paralysed his efficient action, he saw quite distinctly the Venus immortal crossing the tram tracks." If Hueffer, with all his insistence on precise and veridical rendering of realities, could himself have been given to visionary experience, surely Pound cannot have felt any conflict between phatasmagoric activities and his "poetry of reality." He must on the contrary have felt the profundity of his observation about modern men who have had visions of gods: "These things are for them *real*."

---

[17]*Instigations of Ezra Pound*, 234. Cf. the remark quoted in the preceding note about illumination and the *Paradiso* with the later statement: "Dante's 'Paradiso' is the most wonderful *image*" (*Gaudier-Brzeska*, 86: from the 1914 "Vorticism" essay). In a letter to Joyce of March 17, 1917 Pound indicated that he thought of *The Cantos* as originally Imagistic or phanopoeic: "I have begun an endless poem, of no known category. Phanopoeia or something or other, all about everything. 'Poetry' may print the first three cantos this spring." See *Pound/Joyce: The Letters of Ezra Pound to James Joyce, with Pound's Essays on Joyce*, ed. Forrest Read (New York, 1967), 102. Read concludes from this statement that "Phanopoeia" was Pound's original provisional title for *The Cantos*.

[18]In "Pound and Yeats: The Question of Symbolism"; cf. *Letters*, 25.

A History of Pound's Cantos
I-XVI, 1915-1925

This essay will attempt to trace the composition of the early Cantos, the first part of the poem described in 1908 as "that great forty year epic,"[1] from the time Ezra Pound began to compose them in 1915 to their publication in *A Draft of XVI Cantos* in 1925. An examination of Pound's search for a definition of the poem's form may help us to understand the kind of poem *The Cantos* is.

Since the author's worksheets and early drafts are obviously not available, his path must be followed in his published and unpublished letters, and in the published versions of the early Cantos, measured against the London edition of *Seventy Cantos*,[2] which will be considered here as the definitive text of the poem.

If the lines quoted from "Scriptor Ignotus" are evidence of Pound's rather than of his persona's intention, he intended, almost from the beginning of his career, to write an epic. I have, however, found no other significant references to the actual task of writing a long poem until after Pound had received — late in 1913 — Ernest Fenollosa's notes for the translations of the Japanese Noh plays. These plays first suggested to Pound a possible solution to the problem of constructing a long non-narrative, imagist poem.

In September, 1914, Pound wrote: "I am often asked whether there can be a long imagiste or vorticist poem. The Japanese, who evolved the hokku, evolved also the Noh plays. In the best 'Noh' the whole play may consist of one image. I mean it is gathered about one image. Its unity consists in one image, enforced by movement and music. I see nothing against a long vorticist poem."[3] Two years later, after he had already tried to write long poems, he repeated this statement in more specific terms: "These plays are

Reprinted from *American Literature*, XXXV (1963), 183-95, by permission of the author and Duke University Press. Letters by Ezra Pound, first published in Myles Slatin, "A History of Pound's Cantos I-XVI, 1915–1925;" *American Literature*, XXXV (1963). Copyright © 1963 by Ezra Pound. Reprinted by permission of New Directions Publishing Corporation for The Committee for Ezra Pound and Yale University Library.
[1]"Scriptor Ignotus," l.7, *A Lume Spento* (Venice, 1908), p. 26.
[2]London: Faber & Faber, 1950.
[3]"Vorticism," *Fortnightly Review*, n.s. CII, 461-471 (Sept., 1914), reprinted in *Gaudier-Brzeska: A Memoir* (London and New York, 1916), p. 109.

also an answer to a question that has several times been put to me:
'Could one do a long Imagiste poem, or even a long poem in vers
libre?' "[4]

Some eight months or so after he had first proposed the Noh as
a model for a long poem, Pound sent what was intended to be the
first instalment of an epic poem to H. L. Mencken; it was a narrative and it was not in vers libre. The instalment, "L'Homme Moyen
Sensuel," is a satire in which the meter and rhyme imitate "English
Bards and Scotch Reviewers" and the form imitates *Don Juan.* In
the letter accompanying the manuscript, Pound told Mencken he
could "turn you out an installment every two or three months," a
concession to the conditions under which Mencken was operating:
"A long, really long narrative like *Juan* is probably the best, but I
am perfectly willing to recognize the exigencies of the *S*[*mart*]
S[*et*] and make each rip self-contained, as this one is."[5]

"L'Homme Moyen Sensuel" of course is not modeled upon the
Noh, but it does predict both the social comment of *The Cantos* and
the mode of its appearance, in instalments. This letter also makes it
clear that Pound was, at this stage, thinking of his epic in traditional narrative terms. While it may be somewhat surprising that
he should have begun by attempting to imitate *Don Juan*, in many
ways Byron's epic is an appropriate model, for, like *The Cantos*,
Don Juan is at war with conventional linear structure.

Mencken's rejection of "L'Homme Moyen Sensuel" did not lead
its author to abandon the long poem. On May 23, 1915, Pound told
his mother he was "working on a long poem."[6] On June 30 he told
his father he had "sent two long poems to U.S.A., one to *Others* and
one to *Poetry*" (*YC*, No. 393). None of these poems is identifiable,
but one of them may have been "Near Perigord," which appeared in
Poetry in December, 1915. On September 25, 1915, Pound said he

---

[4]*'Noh' or Accomplishment: A Study of the Classical Stage of Japan*, by Ernest
Fenollosa and Ezra Pound (London, 1916), p. 45, n. I.
[5]*The Letters of Ezra Pound, 1907-1941*, ed. D. D. Paige (New York, 1950), p.
58. Hereinafter referred to as *L*.
[6]Yale Collection of American Literature, Letters of Ezra Pound, No. 319, p. I.
This letter is part of a collection of carbon copies, photostats, and films of
more than two thousand letters written by Pound, collected and copied by D.
D. Paige for his edition of *The Letters of Ezra Pound, 1907-1941* and pur-
chased by Yale from Mr. Paige. The great bulk of these letters, hereinafter
referred to as *YC*, remain unpublished. Permission to quote from the unpublished letters or to quote unpublished portions of letters already published by
Mr. Paige has kindly been granted to me by the Yale University library and
by "Mrs. Dorothy Pound, Committee for Ezra Pound." I have retained
Pound's wording and spelling as transcribed by Mr. Paige. Wherever a letter
has been published I have referred to the published text.

was "at work on a very long poem" (*YC*, No. 398, p. 1). This reference may be to the beginning of *The Cantos*.

The first unmistakable reference to the poem which was to become *The Cantos* comes in a letter written on December 18, 1915, as Pound thanks his father for his praise of "Near Perigord": "If you like the 'Perigord' you would probably like Browning's *Sordello*. . . . You'll have to read it sometime as my big long endless poem that I am now struggling with, starts off with a barrelfull of allusions to *Sordello* which will intrigue you if you haven't read the other." *Sordello*, he said, was "A great work and worth the trouble of hacking it out. I began to get it on about the 6th reading. . . ." In his next paragraph Pound defined the basic unit of his poem as the canto and told his father how much he had finished:

> I must have the lot typed out and send it to you as a much belated Xmas [present]. Though I dare say the present version needs a lot done to it. It will be two months at least before I can send it, I suppose, as I don't want to muddle my mind now in the Vth Canto by typing the first three cantos, and I don't want to leave the only copy with a typist while I'm out of town. Besides you may as well have a shot at Sordello first. (*YC*, No. 406, pp. 2-3.)

Parenthetically, it should be noted that on its first appearance, in the June, 1917, *Poetry*, Canto I began: "Hang it all, there can be but one Sordello!" It is plain that by December, 1915, Pound had exchanged Byron for Browning as a guide.

Pound's first reference to *The Cantos* does not announce his design or plan or subject. Indeed, the only passages which may be said to describe the poem at all are those which relate it to *Sordello* and call it "big long endless." The last of these adjectives was repeated a little more than a year later. Writing to John Quinn in January, 1917, Pound said he had begun *The Cantos* after he had finished his work on the Noh; he stressed the endlessness of his poem: "Then came proofs of *Noh*, and then work on a new long poem (really L O N G, endless, leviathanic)" (*L*, p. 104). Although the adjective may be intentional hyperbole, "endless" may well be taken literally: at this stage of its composition the poem had only a beginning; its ending could not be, or had not been, foreseen. So far, the poem was infinite, stretching far forward into time. If Pound did foresee the ending, he did not mention or discuss it, and his language will not support a conclusion that he knew, when he began *The Cantos*, how or when the poem would end.

By December, 1915, he had apparently been working at the problem for some time and had made some progress. He had moved away from satire and its fairly straight chronological and logical plot progression toward the associational, a-chronological thematic progression of *Sordello*; one could almost say that he had moved from the structural principle of narrative *cum* digression of *Don Juan* to the structural principle of narrative *qua* digression on which *Sordello* is built. At the same time — perhaps because of his own difficulties with his long poem — Pound had moved for his model to a poem directly concerned with the relationship between poetry, society, and social power, directly concerned with the poet's role in history, directly concerned with the nature of poetry itself. A poet struggling to create a new language and a new form, Sordello is torn between his power over language and his power over men, and dies as the result of his inability to resolve the dichotomy between language and action. Pound's poem is a direct attempt to resolve this dichotomy as a part of the effort all modern poets have made to achieve the reintegration of modern man.

It is impossible to tell just when Pound did finish a first draft of the Cantos he had announced in December, 1915; the letter in which he tells his father they are coming lacks a precise date. Mr. Paige marks it simply "1917?": "Heres the first 3 cantos of the long poem. . . . I don't want you to show it about until it's printed, or until I have decided on the final form of some of this" (*YC*, No. 447).

Except for this letter, Pound said nothing about the composition of his still untitled long poem until June, 1916. In April, 1916, he told his mother he was "doing some 'Noh' of my own; don't know that they'll ever get finished" (*YC*, No. 416). As the letter cited above to John Quinn indicates, this work was related to the work on *The Cantos:* when he sent the manuscript of the first three Cantos to Harriet Monroe, he told her that their "theme is roughly the theme of 'Takasago,' which story I hope to incorporate more explicitly in a later part of the poem."[7]

---

[7] A microfilm copy in the Yale Collection of American Literature of an undated letter from Ezra Pound to Harriet Monroe in the Harriet Monroe collection of the University of Chicago Library. *Takasago* is one of the "god-plays" or *waki*-No and is one of the plays described in Fenollosa's "Notebook J, Section I," in *'Noh' or Accomplishment*, pp. 9-12; see especially p. 11. *Takasago* is cited in the passage to which footnote 4 above refers, where Pound says that the Nō Plays have "what we may call Unity of Image. At best, the better plays are all built into the intensification of a single Image: The red maple leaves and the snow flurry in Nishikigi, the pines in Takasago, the blue-gray waves and wave pattern in Suma Genji, the mantle of feathers in the play of that name, Hagoromo" (*'Noh' or Accomplishment*, pp. 45-46). Of the four plays in this passage *Takasago* is the only one not printed in 'Noh,' although apparently Fenollosa's notes on the play were available to Pound.

In June, 1916, Pound wrote Harriet Monroe that his "next contribution" would "probably be a 40 page fragment from a more important opus" (*L*, p. 81). The "fragment" took a while to finish, for not until January 4, 1917, could he tell Kate Buss that he was "sending a new thing on to *Poetry* shortly. Perhaps H.M. will print it" (*YC*, No. 449).[8] By March, Pound was wondering whether the fragment he had sent would appear in the April issue of *Poetry* (*L*, p. 108), and a month later he was urging Miss Monroe to print it in any way she liked, just so long as she printed it soon. As Pound had foreseen, she approached the poem with something less than enthusiasm: "string it out into three numbers if that's the best you can do. . . . Only for gawd's sake send it along as soon as possible. Let us hope you may get over your dislike of the poem by the time the last of it is printed" (*L*, p. 110).

The poem was strung out over three numbers: Cantos I, II, and III made their first appearance in print in the June, July, and August, 1917, issues of *Poetry*. This was two and one half years after their composition had been begun; Cantos IV and V, which Pound had been working on in December, 1915, had not yet been submitted. Even allowing for the fact that Pound was always a very busy man, this delay in publication implies that he had not yet found a form which would satisfy him and which would, by establishing a beginning, open the way to the poem's completion.

No sooner had the first three Cantos appeared than Pound began to revise them for the American editions of *Lustra*, published in October, 1917. In August he wrote Miss Monroe that "printing it in three parts has given me a chance to amend, and the version for the book is, I think, much improved" (*L*, p. 115). A comparison of the *Lustra* with the *Poetry* versions will show that the revisions were both extensive and intensive.

These revisions did not satisfactorily solve the problem of finding a suitable beginning for the poem. Except for whatever labor and criticism by excision were involved in making excerpts from these three Cantos for the February, March, and April, 1918, issues of *Future*, Pound did not work again on the poem for nearly two years. Not until 1919 did the poem begin to move forward again; in an undated letter he told his father he was sending "a draft of Fourth Canto, with a few annotations for you. Not to be shown to anyone. . . . Won't be printed until there is another bundle of three; Fifth is begun" (*YC*, No. 519). The *Lustra* text of the first three Cantos

---

[8]This passage was omitted from the published version of this letter (*L*, p. 101).

was apparently to be allowed to stand without revision for the time being. Cantos IV and V of December, 1915, seem to have been scrapped or forgotten, although it is of course possible that this Fourth Canto and the earlier one are the same.

Pound's promise to save the printing of Canto IV until V and VI had been finished was not kept. Canto IV was privately printed by the Ovid Press on October 4, 1919, at about the time that the *Lustra* version of the first three cantos was being reprinted in *Quia Pauper Amavi*.

For the next few months Pound must have felt that he had found the beginning he wanted and that the poem would continue to progress rapidly and smoothly. On November 22, 1919, six weeks after the publication of Canto IV, he asked his father to tell Horace Liveright:

> I have three new cantos done. THUS there is enough matter for American edition of poems, as follows:
> Homage to Propertius
> Langue D'oc
> Moeurs Contemporaines
> Cantos IV, V and VI (possibly VI and VII, by the time matter is settled). (*YC*, No. 536, p. 1)

The volume in question, not to be published until 1921, was *Poems, 1918-21*. The "three new cantos done" must have included the already printed Canto IV, but V and VI meant real progress, as did the fact that VII could be foreseen. The writing of VII took three weeks; on December 13, 1919, Pound announced it to his father: "done cantos 5, 6, 7, each more incomprehensible than the one preceding it" (*YC*, No. 538). Unexpectedly, here the poem stopped; no further reference to the composition of the Cantos seems to have been made until 1922, some three years later.

Although Pound had temporarily stopped writing Cantos, he did not stop publishing them. In June, 1920, Canto IV appeared in the *Dial* in the form it was to take in *Poems 1918-21*. Cantos V, VI, and VII, also in the same version, were printed in the *Dial* in August, 1921, perhaps as part of an effort to arouse interest in their publication in book form. In May, 1922, Canto VIII, not previously referred to, appeared in the *Dial* beginning with a transitional passage, since deleted, linking it to Canto VII. The appearance of this Canto, number II in *Seventy Cantos*, signalled the beginning of another period of intensive work on the long poem. This period, stretching from the spring of 1922 to the early part of 1925, was the

climactic period of the poem's composition, for during it the poem
— or at least the first part of it — took what is now its final shape.

On July 9, 1922, writing to Professor Schelling, Pound was able
to talk as if he had not only finished the first eleven Cantos, but as
if he had some idea of the whole grand design of the poem and could
foresee, however hazily, its ending:

> Perhaps as the poem goes on I shall be able to make various
> things clearer. Having the crust to attempt a poem in 100 or 120
> cantos long after all mankind has been commanded never again to
> attempt a poem of any length, I have to stagger as I can.
>
> The first 11 cantos are preparation of the palette. I *have to* get
> down all the colours or elements I want for the poem. Some perhaps
> too enigmatically and abbreviatedly. I hope, heaven help me, to
> bring them into some sort of design and architecture later. (*L,*
> p. 180)

Although a terminus is mentioned, the second paragraph quoted
makes it plain that Pound was still groping for a design and that,
so far, his work had been part of the process of searching both for
the means of doing what he wanted to do and for the exact nature
of what it was he wanted to do. His palette metaphor indicates
quite clearly that he was still squeezing colors out of the tubes,
choosing, as it were, his spectrum. But the canvas before him was
still blank; perhaps he was hoping, like an action painter, to find his
subject and his form in the vital and intense act of composition.

Five days after this letter, Pound told Kate Buss that he had
"blocked in five more [Am?] Cantos" (*YC*, No. 614).[9] He was
probably counting from Canto VIII and not from Canto IX, for a
month later he wrote his father: "Have now a rough draft of 9, 10,
11, 12, 13. IX may swell out into two" (*YC*, No. 616, p. 1). This
progress was rapid indeed, but the fission of Canto IX was to delay his progress drastically and crucially; only after he had gone
through the struggle to shape these next Cantos was Pound able
to reshape all he had so far done and really begin his work on
the poem.

Canto IX was a Malatesta Canto. On August 20 Pound wrote his
mother that he had "various material for my Malatesta canto lying
about" (*YC*, No. 619). Apparently he was still doing research, still
selecting material he would use, without yet knowing just how he
would use it. On September 2 he was "plugging along on my Mala-

---

[9]The word in brackets was supplied by Mr. Paige; the question mark is mine.

testa Canto, may run into two Cantos; the four to follow it are blocked in" (*YC*, No. 621). If this statement means anything, it means that after six weeks of work he had not gotten beyond IX, was still undecided whether or not he would make one Canto or two out of it, and had settled the later Cantos in rough, not in detail. He did at least have the design of part of his poem.

On October 3 he was "plugging along on my Malatesta cantos; will take years and years and years at the present rate" (*YC*, No. 623). He had made some progress; definitely there would be more than one Malatesta canto. By October 30, he was still "plugging" but he seems to have gotten past Malatesta: "Am plugging on my next batch of cantos. Don't know what else is to be expected of me during the oncoming years" (*YC*, No. 625). By December, although he was not yet quite finished with the Malatesta material, the fission process was continuing, and an image of a sort was emerging from the pigment: "Have got three of the Malatesta cantos into some sort of shape; attempt to avoid going away [for a vacation] with huge mass of notes. Don't know how many more will be needed to deal with S. M.; several cantos blocked in, to follow the Malatesta section" (*YC*, No. 626). What was in question was not, apparently, the design of the whole, but the size of this particular item; Pound still did not know, some four months after he had begun dealing with the Malatesta material, how large a portion of the poem it would occupy. However, the poem was moving forward faster and farther than it ever had, for if, by December, 1922, the ninth Canto had turned into three, then by that Christmas he had rough drafts of at least fifteen Cantos.

How long Pound's vacation lasted, and when he finished the Malatesta Cantos, I cannot tell. The next reference to work on the poem comes on June 6, 1923, some six months later, when he told his mother he was "working on Kung canto" (*YC*, No. 639). This Canto is most probably the one now numbered XIII. Fifteen days later, Pound was still working on it: "I'm doing a canto on Kung; don't know about English translations of him. I have Pauthier's French translation of the *Four Books* and a Latin translation of the *Odes. . .*" (*YC*, No. 640, p. 1). While he was working on the Kung Canto, Pound was also busy with others: on the second page of this same letter, he says he has other Cantos, besides the Malatesta group, "lying here on desk unfinished. Including Hell and the Honest Sailor" (p. 2). These may be fragments of the Cantos he had said were done in rough draft in August, 1922, for the Hell Cantos are now Cantos XIV and XV and the story of the Honest Sailor is in the present Canto XII. This letter may be taken to indicate that what I have considered to be a basic indecision about the design of the poem may be something else: a holding of the design in solution until enough pieces had been gathered so that the design might become visible.

Before the summer of 1923 began, the Malatesta Cantos were finished; they were published under that title as "Cantos IX to XII of a Long Poem" in the July *Criterion*. One Canto had swelled into four, but the work on this part of the poem proved satisfactory; with only some minor changes in lineation and spelling, these four Cantos now appear as Cantos VIII-XI. But what is more important, the design of the poem suddenly crystallized, perhaps partly as a result of the long and intensive labor which went into the Malatesta group. Within a month or perhaps two months of the publication of these Cantos, Pound had entirely revised the beginning of the poem and had come to the end of the composition of the first sixteen Cantos.

On August 24, 1923, Pound told his father he had "knocked some more Canti into shape, now on fifth on from Malatesta, and have revised earlier part of the poem" (*YC*, No. 642.) What this meant is more explicitly stated in a letter apparently written in July but put by Mr. Paige after the letter just quoted: "Have finished canto XVI, that is fifth after the Malatesta, having rewritten beginning of poem and condensed three cantos into two" (*YC*, No. 643).[10]

From this letter, unfortunately, one cannot tell whether Pound had actually, during this summer, put the early Cantos into the shape they wore when they were next published or had merely condensed them without changing the position of various pieces of the poem. The latter may be the safer guess, although the former is the more tempting. However, it seems significant that only after he had finished the Malatesta group was Pound able to rethink the poem sufficiently to change drastically those parts of it left untouched since the appearance of the *Lustra* volumes.

Although Canto XVI had been announced as done, the announcement did not necessarily mean that Pound had either completely finished it or had established the final form of the other Cantos. In January, 1924, fragments of two Cantos were published under the

---

[10]It is difficult to tell which of these letters should come first. Since Pound had a habit of forgetting what he had told his parents, the month assigned to No. 643 by Mr. Paige may well be correct. However, the completion of Canto XVI announced in No. 643 should mean that this letter, in spite of its July date, was written after No. 642.

title, "Two Cantos."[11] The first was the Canto now numbered XIII, with the present lines 3-6 omitted, and the second consisted of the first 76 lines (except for the present line 38) of what is now Canto XII. That these should appear without numbers may indicate that Pound had not yet determined where these fragments belonged. Pound may have deliberately withheld parts of these Cantos so that they might first appear in book form; he told his father on January 29, 1924, that "There is a hell (2 cantos) & war (one canto) & the honest sailor ½ of that canto. That you haven't yet seen — reserved for the book" (*YC*, No. 655, p. 1). The book for which these pieces were being saved was, of course, *A Draft of XVI Cantos*, which had not yet gone to press, but which had been in preparation since at least as early as May, 1923, when Pound told his mother that The Three Mountains Press was preparing a "de looks edtn. of Malatesta" (*YC*, No. 636).

There are no references in the letters to further work on the Cantos until May, 1924; presumably, during February, March, and April, Pound was busy putting the first sixteen cantos into shape for printing. We are told on page [67] of *A Draft of XVI Cantos* that the book was printed between May and December; it is not unlikely that Pound took three months to settle the text of the poem. By January 28, 1925, when he acknowledged the receipt of a proof copy of the whole book (*YC*, No. 719), the early part of the poem had been given the form in which it is now known.

By this date the passage from the Nekuia, which had come at the end of Canto III in August, 1917, was moved to the place of honor in Canto I. The Canto which had been published in May, 1922, as Canto VIII was moved into position as Canto II; the Kung Canto was given its number, XIII, and lines 3-6 of the present text added; line 38 was added to Canto XII and the story of the Honest Sailor given its rightful place alongside Baldy Bacon; the war and hell Cantos were put into place. In other words, between the summer of 1923 and the spring of 1924, the scattered pieces of the Cantos fell into order; the architecture of what once had been referred to as the palette became plain. The structural key was provided, almost inadvertently, by the Malatesta group, but once the organizing historical principle had been found, what had existed potentially came into being.

Now that the first sixteen Cantos were on their way to print, Pound could move ahead rapidly and even identify in advance the

---

[11]*Transatlantic Review*, I, 10-14 (Jan., 1924).

kinds of materials he would be able to use — something he had been unable to do previously. On May 16, 1924, he told his father he had "read vast work on Ferrara & blocked out course of a few more cantos" (*YC*, No. 679). On May 28, he said he wanted "an almost infinite number of facts to select from" (*YC*, No. 681, p. 1). On June 21 he had "just summarized Marco Polo's note on Kublai Khan's issue of paper currency" (*YC*, No. 684); the summary now occupies lines 1-24 of Canto XVIII. By the end of October he had "shaped up some more cantos; and sent you carbons of two that are more or less finished" (*YC*, No. 697).

A few days later, he was able to see that he had finished his work on one phase of the poem and must begin to cast about for material for the next unit. His procedure and his language make it clear that although he knew in a structural sense what kind of unit he needed, he did not know what he would use. On October 25, 1924, Pound wrote: "Must start on another LONG hunk of Canti, like the Sigismundo, having used up the chop-chop in the five now drafted. (2 of which I have sent you.) . . . . Am using a bit of Jefferson in the XX or thereabouts" (*YC*, No. 698). Apparently, he had reached Canto XXI by using the fragments left over from the research done for the first sixteen. On November 1, 1924, Pound defined what he was looking for: "Have send Dad two cantos; and done more, not yet in shape to send. Am, as I possibly wrote him, ready for another long chunk; and trying to find some bhloomin historic character who can be used as illustration of intelligent constructivity. Private life being another requisite. S[igismundo]. M[alatesta]. amply possessed of both; but other figures being often fatally deficient" (*YC*, No. 700). This statement indicates that Pound was not always entirely open-minded in his approach to history and that at this point he had at least tentatively defined "an underlying purpose or current . . . beneath a series of facts"[12] so that the poem could proceed by a process of recognition.

Like the sculptor looking in the stone for the god he has always known would be there, Pound has continued to work on *The Cantos*. So far as I am aware, his work on the poem, since 1925, has been uninterrupted by difficulties with design. By the time *A Draft of XVI* had been published, the poem had really achieved itself;

---

[12]"Real knowledge goes into natural man in titbits. A scrap here, a scrap there; always pertinent, linked to safety, or nutrition or pleasure. If however an underlying purpose or current cd. be established beneath a series of facts (as is done by Edgar Wallace even in some of his craziest stories) education might be more rapid. Without going to excess?" (*Guide to Kulchur*, Norfolk, Conn., n.d., pp. 99-100).

what remained was the filling in of the details of a design or plan already implicit in the first sixteen cantos. Pound's prose since 1925 has been dedicated to the writing of footnotes to his poem and to an elucidation of it; his prose since then has served the same purpose as the notes he originally published to his dramatic monologues: "To me the short so-called dramatic lyric — at any rate the sort of thing I do — is the poetic part of a drama the rest of which (to me the prose part) is left to the reader's imagination or implied or set in a short note" (*L*, pp. 3-4).

Throughout this early period of the poem's composition Pound made no statements, of which I am aware, which describe the poem's design or intent as a whole, with the highly ambiguous exception of the 1922 letter to Professor Schelling. In fact, there are no attempts before 1927 to explicate a design;[13] as late as 1937 Pound was still paraphrasing what he had told Professor Schelling in 1922: "When I get to end, pattern *ought* to be discoverable" (*L*, p. 293). The absence of a written rationale for the poem does not mean that Pound did not have one; he was certainly under no obligation to write or publish one if he had formulated it, but the process of composition described here does not support the contention that a carefully rationalized structural design existed. When Pound began his poem, he began it, I think, more in the manner of Byron composing *Don Juan* than in the manner of Milton beginning *Paradise Lost*. Though one way is not better than the other, the difference in method seems to indicate a difference in kind.

To borrow Robert Langbaum's term, *The Cantos* is a poem of experience, like *Don Juan* and like so much post-Romantic literature.[14] To use a term from modern art criticism, *The Cantos* is an "action" poem, free to move improvisationally and accidentally in any direction as the process of composition clarifies what is implicit in its material, and in directions which could not possibly have been foreseen at the beginning. Neither the Pisan nor the Chinese Cantos could have been anticipated in 1923, at the moment when Odysseus's visit to the all-seeing Tiresias became the first experience of the poem, yet both the Pisan and the Chinese Cantos are well prepared for by the first Canto.

13See *L*, p. 210.

14"The disequilibrium between the completeness of the flow of consciousness or life, and the incompleteness of the events that rise out of the flow and sink back into it, gives to literature a new shape — a shape by which the poetry of experience can be identified" (Robert Langbaum, *The Poetry of Experience: The Dramatic Monologue in Modern Literary Tradition*, London, 1957, p. 227).

Prediction is always hazardous, and perhaps the only thing which can be foretold about the ending of *The Cantos* is that it will come. The final Cantos may show us Dioce and so clarify all, but Dioce, or a Dioce, has always been there. I do not think we need it to show us the shape and size and meaning of the picture; there is a sense in which the poem's meanings have already been given, its mysteries revealed. It is nevertheless true that the ending of the poem may make a major difference as the final piece of the design clarifies and perfects what has gone before, as once more Pound unfolds what we have been too blind to see. But in a poem dedicated to and modeled upon experience there can, in one very powerful sense, be no ending, as there can be no ending to experience. Like Melville's Ishmael, experience ends and then bobs up to the surface again to go on; Odysseus, with whom *The Cantos* begins, must, one journey finished, begin again, oar on his shoulder.

Michael Alexander

On Rereading *The Cantos*

We have in the last few years had too many works of exegesis on *The Cantos* of Ezra Pound. Mr Pound noted (in Canto 96) that "if we never write anything save what is already understood, the field of understanding will never be extended." Whether or not *The Cantos* will ultimately succeed in pushing back the frontiers of unenlightenment, the surface of the poem itself is disfigured by the mole-hills of source-snoops and allusion-identifiers. The mystical attitude of Charles Olson and Co. seems equally unhelpful. To provide something of more general interest for this number, I have in the last week reread *The Cantos* as far as Canto 109, the end of *Thrones*. This short piece consists of some untechnical reflections occasioned by my rereading.

Reprinted from *Agenda* (London), IV (October-November 1965), 4-10, Ezra Pound's Eightieth Birthday Issue, by permission of the author and *Agenda*.

Firstly, to clear the ground of the objection to *The Cantos* most frequently voiced in "normal" (as opposed to academic) circles, that they are "obscure" or "above my head" (and yours too), I think one might ask whether the poem would carry conviction if it had praised more conventional heroes? Suppose that for Benito Mussolini we had Winston Churchill; for Sigismundo Malatesta, Cosimo de Medici; for Thomas Jefferson, Abe Lincoln; for the Greek gods, the God of the Christians; for Confucius, Aristotle; for the Antonines and Byzantine emperors, Pericles. The reader's prejudices and preconceptions would not have been ruffled; and he would not care to admit that he was in reality as hazy about the popular as the unpopular figures.

One's first impression of *The Cantos* themselves is, as before, not of the method of composition or the unique subject-matter, but of sheer beauty of style. Whatever vicissitudes Mr Pound's reputation may suffer in years to come, no one will I think seek to deny the affirmation of his fellow-practitioners, from Yeats to Eliot to William Carlos Williams, that Ezra Pound has the finest possible ear for the rhythms of the spoken word. This carries one through almost everything, whether or not one agrees with or understands it. And one's interest is given constant renewal and delight by the clear language, from such simplicity as

> Behind hill the monk's bell
> borne on the wind

and the whole of that Canto (XLIX), to the 'chopped prose' of Canto XXXIII

> 'Is that despotism
> or absolute power . . . unlimited sovereignty,
> is the same in a majority of a popular assembly,
> an aristocratical council, an oligarchical junto,
> and a single emperor, equally arbitrary, bloody,
> and in every respect diabolical. Wherever it has resided, etc. . .'

One might add here that the easy preference so frequently expressed by newspaper reviewers for the passages of great lyric beauty in *The Pisan Cantos* and elsewhere *over* the 'chopped prose' of the Jefferson cantos, the Leopoldine reforms, the Chinese section and the Adams cantos seems to be due to the fact that the said reviewers, having many books to read and few column inches to fill, object to finding out whether what Mr Pound maintains is in fact the case, which would involve a lot of homework. There is nothing wrong with the *style* of the history cantos, which when I read them through, were fully as varied, inventive, and cleanly worded as the lyric passages, and often had more 'attack'.

I found, then, that *The Cantos* constantly renewed my interest by their style; whether lyric, narrative, gnomic, elegiac or mixed, the matter is completely, clearly stated. All the talk of technique may have made people think Pound an aesthete, a lingerer over niceties: not at all, his technique is one of efficient delivery of the sense. There it is, solid, 'perdurable'. Mr Pound need have no worries as to whether he has stated his case; he has.

With the increase of 'Pound studies', with the *Pound Newsletter*, with the book which tracked down *every reference* in the work, we have come to take *The Cantos* rather for granted, as if it were as over and done with as the Epic of Gilgamesh and simply waiting to be dissected and lectured on. Yet one cannot read straight through the work, as yet unfinished, without a feeling of astonishment similar to that experienced by anyone who went to the Picasso Exhibition in London of a few years ago. *The Cantos* are a phenomenon, a prodigious performance of the human imagination; now totalling 809 pages (in my editions). They have been 'in progress' for half a century. And when one remembers the circumstances of the author for twelve of those fifty or so years, the dedication necessary to this task speaks through the statistics. Mr Pound, unlike a hated predecessor in the field of the epic poem in English, does not announce at the beginning that the Cantos encompass 'things unattempted yet in prose or rime'; but they do. The range and scale of the poem impress themselves upon the reader, as do the energy and curiosity of Mr Pound's mind, the richness of his reading and the variety of his interests and his modes of expression. Though his poem is of the past, he concentrates, at his best and most characteristic on what is *living* in the past.

The scale and intensity of this great enterprise, then, impress the reader deeply, and will, I think, continue to do so always. But (to come to a crucial point) what is its purpose? It is not, certainly, to justify the works of God to man (Mr Pound mistrusts the 'original sin racket'), or to sing the anger of Achilles, or arms and the man. Mr Pound began, at least, with trying to write an epic; but we must not criticise *The Cantos* if we find them different from Milton's or anyone else's idea of an epic. Epic intention is clear in Canto I, that mysterious and impressive overture, where Odysseus goes down to the world of the dead to consult the ancient wisdom of Tiresias on how to get home. As has been pointed out, this is what the author himself is to do throughout the poem — he consults Confucius and the Americans, Jefferson and Adams; he raises to life Malatesta and other heroes: he moves with the gods. The parallel with the *Commedia* of Dante is also strong (the going down to hell, the moral judgement of people in history and of the present day, the spiritual ascent); and again Mr Pound's life parallels Alighieri's exile. But both Homer and Dante tell a story; Mr Pound does not. The choice was not really a free one: an epic poem demands that the audience should share the poet's view of the world in its essentials, that they should both believe in a mythic non-temporal history of the world and of the tribe, that they should recognize the same heroes and the same virtues, that public life should have meaning and public actions be capable of being seen in a heroic light. It is not so much that Mr Pound eschewed a story, the age (the only 'epic' historian in England today is Arthur Bryant) denied him one. 'The age demanded', we know, that Mr Pound go away and write his epic someplace else. The public/private split between state and artist, glaringly manifest today (the story of President Johnson getting his staff to find a passage in Robert Lowell's writing which he might introduce into a speech so as to placate the poet; and of the staff providing a quote from James Russell Lowell), is not Mr Pound's fault.

The saddle Homer rode, then, is still vacant. *The Cantos* are no epic in any strict sense: there is no story, no conflict of character and event (except in the case of the author's own odyssey). There *is* nobility, there *is* a heroic dimension to Odysseus, to Sigismundo, to Kung, to Vidal, to Jefferson, to el Cid, to John Randolph of Roanoke, to de Maensac, to the dynamic men of action celebrated throughout *The Cantos*; and Mussolini is presented in such a way that it makes one sure that the current British caricature of him as the lieutenant of the devil incarnate is badly out. The strong men, the explorers, the founders, come through as heroes all right. But Adams does not in the same way as de Maensac or Confucius' father (a thumbnail sketch of 'character isolated by a deed') despite the ten Cantos devoted to him; and with the Chinese, Roman or Byzantine emperors one does not know whether one admires them or not, because they are not individuals, unlike the 'glorious bandits' such as Bertran de Born and others in Mr Pound's Valhalla. The bandits (Ruy Diaz, Malatesta, Randolph) beat the emperors (Antoninus, Leopold of Siena, etc) all ends up; it is dynamic vs. static, Robin Hood vs. the Sheriff of Nottingham.

But how do the emperors get in? The epic, Mr Pound wrote long
ago, is a poem containing history. Yes, but what sort of history?
Mr Pound was surely right when he said that Shakespeare's history plays were the English epic. But Shakespeare's history is
mythological, not economic. Its relation to fact is that of the oak
to the acorn; Richard III (research apparently reveals) was *not* a
hunchback and was in fact a good king who got a bad press. But
mythopoiea is stronger than mere fact, and nobody is interested in
'the real' Richard III. Mr Pound's emperors, his exemplars of recti-
tude, showed in real life a moral courage equal to the more romantic
courage of the men of action; we may respect and even admire
them; indeed, Mr Pound makes us do so. But they are figures in a
pageant, in a tapestry. Mr Pound has not 'thought of them living'
as he did the troubadours in *Provincia Deserta*. Their presence in
the poem is not unwelcome (though Mussolini, bandit and emperor,
seems a dubious exemplar of 'order' and 'brotherly deference');
indeed, Jefferson is one of the great successes of the poem, a truly
inspiring characterization.

The emperors and the heroes shine before us in their appointed
places. But what of the economic history? What place has that in
an epic? What have interest rates to do with nobility? There is a
connection, though not perhaps such a direct one as is made out by
Mr Pound; but the harping on that connection seems almost obses-
sive. I have taken the trouble to read Mr Pound's economics books
and think to have understood them. Even if he were right — and
there is more moral sense in his views than is usually allowed —
documentation should surely not occupy such a large place in an
epic. Despite the Leopoldine cantos and the Usura cantos which
follow them (all as fascinating and as skillful as the rest of the
poem) much of the statistical detail forms a body of less distinguished writing which stands out in the midst of so much spendour
and sense.

Many critics give every sign of being baffled by the presence of
the economics in the poem at all. But it is far from inexplicable:
the attitude of the author of *The Cantos* to usury is a moral one —
it is the same as that of William Langland and of Chaucer as well
as those cited in the poem. Mr Pound believes in social justice and
in a fair deal for men who do productive work; he believes that
money should be a measure of value; that there should be a stable
relationship between wage and price; he believes that true wealth
is from the abundance of nature utilized by the skill of man. He
finds it scandalous that money should be a commodity whose value

is regulated by a few men sitting on their backsides in Wall Street or Threadneedle Street, as, broadly speaking, it might seem to have been until the disaster of the thirties. For Mr Pound fiscal policy is a touchstone of the good faith of the government.

This argument seems to have escaped the majority of critics — though how this can have come about I do not know. A moral idealistic attitude towards foreign policy is quite common among liberal journalists of the sort who laugh at the economics of *The Cantos*; but they seem to regard the mechanics of the whole internal system of the country as unworthy of their consideration. Mr Pound reasserts the right of the individual to examine the accounts of his elected government; and the defenders of democracy are horrified. The propriety of these views seems to me incontestable but the propriety of devoting such a large part of *The Cantos* to them seems to me dubious in theory and more than dubious in effect. In theory it was a good idea to cross the epic with the satire; since *Don Juan* English poetry had gone soft, had retreated into the vicarage garden. Mr Pound refused to acquiesce in the silent expropriation of the public realm and in the exclusion of anger from the range of emotions proper to a poet. He thought he saw what had "bitched" the "natural order" of society and was optimistic enough to think that to expose the guilty party might help to restore that precious balance of the empires of the past in which the citizen and the artist could flourish in peace; I am afraid that his enlightened opinion of mankind is unwarrantable. Certainly his villains attract from him more heat than light. His moral point of view not accepted, his insistence grew greater; one can see it growing in *The Cantos*. So to Canto 52 the presentation of the case is clear, and even if we don't agree with it, we can accept its place in the poem. But thereafter the "evidence" seemed to me repetitious and the indignation less focussed. From these strictures one might except the history, as opposed to the economics, while minuting the practical query as to how the bandits would have survived under the emperors.

How do these considerations affect the unity of *The Cantos*? That is perhaps the most important question of all. My rereading confirmed me in my opinion that one must abandon the claim that *The Cantos* have a complete and objective unity, coherence and validity; *The Cantos have* a genuine coherence, and one is sensible of it when reading them through. But it is a subjective unity, the unity of a unique mind voyaging through human history and finding paradisal havens, thrones. Mr Pound *does* succeed in objectifying his vision in *The Pisan Cantos*, where his earthly paradise is, in fragments, 'fairly tough and unblastable'; there he succeeds in universalizing his perceptions. But in general, Mr Pound's renunciation of traditional structure and logical rhetoric must be said to have made his poem a series of lyric celebrations and Blasts rather than an epic.

This is not to forget that *The Cantos* have been for myself and many others an open sesame to whole historical epochs and whole literatures which might otherwise have remained closed. These men and these periods, though, are alive because we see them with Mr Pound's eyes; and when they write or speak, the voice is the voice of Ezra. We are privileged in *The Cantos* to share his vision of human history as a living whole, in which, like Dante, we can move freely. But ironically, though he has rigidly excluded himself from the poem as someone of no interest, and though he always will quote another rather than give his own opinion, it is the poet himself in the persona of Odysseus, who becomes the hero of the poem. I am sure that this was contrary to Mr Pound's intention, and he may not be pleased at this interpretation; but it is one which has forced itself on me, and it is one which is half admitted in the Cantos subsequent to the Pisan sequence. It is precisely with the Pisan sequence that one becomes directly conscious of the poet's presence in his poem, playing Virgil to the reader's Dante. After the Kung and Adams Cantos the personal voice is heard; even those who do not like *The Cantos* testify to the moving power of these remarkable pages. Mr Pound's courage and *hilaritas* shine out, and all the many threads of the poem are drawn together again; the barbed wire cage seems to contain the poetic mind of Europe, and as reminiscence of Yeats and Ford mingle with the sight of the birds on the telephone wires and the beauty of common daylight, the 'fugue' method of juxtaposition becomes quite natural, and takes on a larger rhythm and a stricter formal organization. This new accent and this jewel-like concentration never entirely leave the poem from that point. In *Thrones* the incredibly deft and accurate delineation of physical beauty seem, if anything, even more refined than before; and the poet, never characterising himself other than by the tone of his voice, seems to be approaching some illumination.

To sum up on *The Cantos* so far, one can safely say that in technical accomplishment and variety of invention they rank with the best long poems in the language. One may also say that no long poem of comparable seriousness or intensity has been written since *The Prelude*. The heroic intensity of the vision makes the poem a more subjective one than Mr Pound intended; it also marks (as it seems to me) the mirror of truth with facts that may be right or wrong. But this tactical error was dictated by the same powerful creative mind and the same high personal standards which make *The Cantos* a noble and permanent achievement.

In a published fragment of Canto 115 Mr Pound writes

> Let the Gods forgive what I have made
> Let those I love try to forgive what I have made

This humility in a great man once so certain of his axes of judgement and of the criteria which allowed him to write his vision in words which are often *aere perennius*, is surprising and moving. Odysseus has not lost "all companions": there are readers in the *piccioletta barca*. We hope that a new decad of cantos embodying the change evident in the lines quoted above may come to fruition. A large company wish to Mr Pound on his birthday all health and every happiness.

Walter Baumann

"Perennial War" in *The Cantos*

If Pound's *Cantos* is rightly called an epic, we might expect to find, as in most epics, an initial declaration like Virgil's "arma virumque cano," stating clearly what the poet is above all going to sing of. In vain do we look for this at the beginning of Pound's epic. We suddenly find it, however, in the *Rock-Drill* Cantos:

> Bellum cano perenne . . .
>   . . .   between the usurer and any man who
>   wants to do a good job
>   (perenne).[1]

Reprinted from *The Rose in the Steel Dust: An Examination of The Cantos of Ezra Pound* (Coral Gables, Fla.: University of Miami Press, 1970), pp. 164–72, by permission of the author.

[1] 86:28, continued, from the second line, in 87:29; cf. the echoes in 88:39, 88:41 and 100:65f. Stock used this modified form as the motto of *Impact*: "Bellum cano perenne, between usura and the man/who wants to do a good job." [*Impact: Essays on Ignorance and the Decline of American Civilization*, ed. Noel Stock (Chicago: Henry Regnery, 1960).]

If war and strife are taken as *the* characteristic subject of epic, to speak of the struggle between the usurer-exploiter and the honestly striving individual as a "perennial war" is to make this subject epic indeed, especially since Pound employs the historical method to depict it and since he holds that "an epic is a poem containing history."[2]

This may very well serve as one description of the principal subject of *The Cantos* and of Pound's own personal struggle. Up to Canto XLV, as Pound himself said in the BBC Broadcasts, the poem was a kind of detective story where one was trying to find the crime. Yet how has investigation of usurious practices come to take up so much of Pound's energy, why has he spent so many years of his life "on this case / first case" to "set down part of / The Evidence" (46:28/245), asking in his capacity as investigator the question:

> "Can we take this into court?
> "Will any jury convict on this evidence?
>
>   . . .
>
>   will any
>   JURY convict 'um?   (46:27/243)

(meaning the usurers). "Whatever economic passions I now have," we know Pound to have said in 1933, "begin *ab initio* from having crimes against living art thrust under my perceptions." (*Impact*, p. 88) If this were his only reason, we might with little hesitation call him an intellectual snob.[3]

Having struck people in 1912 as possessing "gno bolidigal basshunts",[4] he has himself been inclined to assume that, although he could not "say exactly where [his] study of government started," "the *New Age* office helped [him] to see the war as a separate event

---

[2]Donald Hall, "The Art of Poetry V: Ezra Pound," *Paris Review*, 28 (Summer/Fall, 1962), p. 47 (hereafter *Paris Review*); *Impact*, p. 142.

[3]Cf.: "But in his general criticism of the present age, especially in his attacks on 'the present accounting system' and on 'monetary inflation,' there is little more than a smartly expressed indignation at the relationship between culture and money." (Heinrich Straumann, *American Literature in the 20th Century* [1962], p. 197).

[4]It was Dr. Henry Slominsky (see John H. Edwards and William W. Vasse, *Annotated Index to the Cantos of Ezra Pound* [Berkeley and Los Angeles: University of California Press, corrected edition, 1959]) who said this to Pound, judging by the mimicry, with a heavy German accent. Cf.: "Slovinsky [sic] looked at me in 1912: 'Boundt, haff you gno bolidigal basshuntz?' " (Typically Poundian phonetics for "no political passions?" See *Impact*, p. 88.)

but as part of a system, one war after another".[5] Here, coming from
his association with Major C. H. Douglas and A. R. Orage, is an
entirely different emphasis, one on political economy, responsible,
also, for his admiration for Mussolini. Here he found, at any rate,
the basis which he thought his fellow-poets were singularly lacking:

> But the lot of 'em, Yeats, Possum and Wyndham
> had no ground beneath 'em
> Orage had.[6]

Apart from the fact that his interest in the issue of money may
have been to a certain extent hereditary, as his grandfather, T. C.
Pound, "had already in 1878 been writing about, or urging among
his fellow Congressmen, the same essentials of monetary and statal
economics"[7] as Pound was writing about during World War II, he
has come to hold that "monetary theory is worthy of study because
it leads us to the contemplation of justice" (*Impact*, p. 69). As long
as there is no "just and honest currency," with, preferably, "state
authority behind it" (*Impact*, p. 94), "the real aim of Law [which
is] to prevent coercion, either by force or by fraud" (BBC), cannot
be achieved. Hence he believes that unless man conquers his "ignorance of coin, credit, and circulation," his real enemy (V. *Impact*, p.
109), he will never see that the usurers' "technique is two lies at
once,"[8] and he will never enjoy proper justice. Economics, in this
light, is not "a cold thing"; if he refuses to be moved by it[9] he will
never acquire the knowledge "sans which a loss of freedom is con-
sequent," this knowledge and safeguard being "monetary literacy"
(103:84). The struggle between the exploiter and the individual is
thus part of a more comprehensive one, "the struggle for individual

---

[5]*Paris Review*, 28, 41.

[6]98:37; cf. 102:80. The Chinese character indicates incompleteness. See
Pound's obituary, "In the Wounds: Memoriam A. R. Orage," in *Impact*, pp.
157–165. Cf. also: "Thus Orage respected belatedly" (104:94).

[7]*Impact*, p. 65. On the dubiety of his grandfather's paper scrip money used by
his own Lumbering Company see Charles Norman, *Ezra Pound* (New York:
Macmillan, 1960), pp. 234f and 351.

[8]100:69. Stock writes: "After many years of study he came to the conclusion
that monetary manipulation could be reduced to variations on the following
'rackets': (1) the lending of that which is made out of nothing; and (2) the
alteration of the value of the monetary unit." (Noel Stock, *Poet in Exile. Ezra
Pound* [Manchester: The University Press, 1964], p. 192.)

[9]Cf.: "Can't move 'em with/a cold thing like economics" (78:59/512; cf. 103:
87, etc.). This records an observation made by the Sinn Fein leader, Arthur
Griffith (cf. Stock, *Poet in Exile*, p. 251).

rights," to which Pound refers specifically as "an epic subject, consecutive from jury trial in Athens to Anselm versus William Rufus,
to the murder of Becket and to Coke and through John Adams."[10]

Although, as Sir Herbert Read has it, 'it is still possible to maintain, with reason and scientific proof, that usury has been the major
cause of misery in the modern world, and that for wickedness one
cannot suggest a rival to those financial and technological monop-
olies that profit from war and the propagations for war,"[11] a discussion of the truth of this and its bearing on Pound's treasonable
broadcasts is inappropriate here. Instead we leave this controversial
subject and focus our attention on that side of Pound's preoccupation with usury which has a long literary tradition.

Since he insists that

> ... the true base of credit ... is
> the abundance of nature[12]

and not gold, we find him truly in the company of Dante, who
placed the usurers next to the sodomites in his hell, of Chaucer, and
not least of Shakespeare, from whom he significantly quotes the
question put to Shylock:

> Or is your gold ... ewes and rams?[13]

What is even more significant is that in the comment following this
Shakespearean fragment the word "usury" — perhaps a misleading
and unhappy metonymy for Pound's monetary concerns anyway —
does not occur, but a far more general statement:

> No! it is not money that is the root of the evil. The root is greed,
> the lust for monopoly. "Captans annonam, maledictus in plebe sit!"

---

[10]*Paris Review*, 28, 48.

[11]*London Magazine* (Aug. 1959), p. 41. From the controversy between H.
Read and C. P. Snow over the latter's Rede Lecture, *The Two Cultures and
the Scientific Revolution*, continued in the issues for October (pp. 57f) and
November (p. 73).

[12]52:3/367. See the founding of the Monte dei Paschi, treated in Cantos
XLII-XLIV and e.g. in *Impact*, pp. 46 & 147; cf. also *Guide*, p. 194, where
Pound calls it, after the Malatesta Cantos, "the second episode." (Ezra
Pound, *Guide to Kulchur* [Norfolk, Conn.: New Directions, 1952].)

[13]The line in *The Merchant of Venice* I, iii, 95 occurs in Antonio's reply to
Shylock's account of Jacob's thriving on sheep. Shylock answers: "I cannot
tell: I Make it breed as fast." Cf. *Guide*, p. 149.

thundered St. Ambrose—"Hoggers of harvest, cursed among the people!" (*Impact*, p. 113)

We need only quote two more comments from *Impact* on gold in order to realize fully that it is nature, in the way a Shakepeare understood it, that Pound has come to accept as the basis of everything:

> Gold is durable, but does not reproduce itself ... It is absurd to speak of it as bearing fruit or yielding interest. Gold does not germinate like grain. To represent gold as doing this is to represent it falsely. (p. 115)

In basing money on gold, man "invented something against nature, a false representation in the mineral world of laws which apply only to animals and vegetables" (p. 112). This is the great error which Pound wants us to understand. Here lies the fatal departure from:

> The plan [which] is in nature (99:61).

Whenever men lapse into such an error, they become victims of that force in history which "divides, shatters, and kills."

The one man who, being in harmony with the other force in history, the "one that contemplates the unity of the mystery" (*Impact*, p. 44), is most likely to have found the wisdom that may "keep them from falling"[14] is Confucius, in his *Ta Hio*, for Pound says about it: "The proponents of a world order will neglect at their peril the study of the only process that has repeatedly proved its efficiency as social coordinate." (*Confucius*, p. 19) Here is, for Pound, the soundest ethical basis the world has yet discovered. If "the process of looking straight into one's heart" is followed, and "what results, i.e. the action resultant from this straight gaze into the heart," is "spread ... thru the people" (85:8), a nation will come "to rest, being at ease in perfect equity" (*Confucius*, pp. 27, 21 & 29).

Confucius, then, has provided Pound with the ethical standards by which the great variety of figures appearing in the *Cantos* are implicitly judged. Their place in Pound's hierarchy of values depends on the degree to which they have acted upon the straight gaze into the heart. In the degree that their hearts are straight (V. 99:54) they bestow treasure on mankind, for "honesty is the trea-

---

[14] 13:60/64. The phrase actually refers to "the blossoms of the apricot," but implied is the Confucian rectification of the heart.

sure of states" (*Confucius*, p. 89), and upon honesty and sincerity civic order may be established and perfected.

What has to be added to Pound's Confucianism to make a description of the centre of the *Cantos* fuller does not actually lead away from Confucius, but merely amplifies his teaching:

> Beyond civic order:
> l'AMOR.   (94:94)

This not only evokes Pound's Neo-Platonism, but also to the very core of Pound. In Pisa he wrote:

> Amo ergo sum, and in just that proportion   (80:71/526).

Even before World War II, he had used the French version of this, "J'ayme donc je suis," printed as a letterhead on his stationery,[15] and in 1942 he had said: "Without strong tastes one does not love, nor, therefore, exist." (*Impact*, p. 69).

Pound asserts:

> That love is the "form" of philosophy,
> is its shape (è forma di Filosofia)
> and that men are naturally friendly
> at any rate from his (Dant's) point of view   (93:86);

and since we philosophize, since "we think because we do not know,"[16] to think is to love, and to love is to perceive with "strong tastes." But this may make us "furious from perception" (104:93) and engender its very opposite, hate, which utterly destroys, if not checked, because it may lead to "a blindness that comes from inside" (104:93). Here is the great tension that has so largely determined Pound's life.

"Patriam quam odi et amo for no uncertain reasons," Pound wrote in 1909 in "What I Feel About Walt Whitman." As long as hate is not allowed to break loose from love, as long as it does not obstruct the "straight gaze into the heart," it is morally justified,

---

[15]Pointed out by Quinn, *Motive & Method in The Cantos of Ezra Pound,* Lewis Leary, ed. (New York: Columbia University Press, 1954), p. 85.

[16]*Impact*, pp. 57 & 74, the second time immediately before the already mentioned palindrome: "R O M A
O   M
M   O
A M O R

because then it is identical with just indignation at what is against nature and the honesty that comes from being in harmony with it, and helps "to know good from evil" (89:50). Then it is the hate operative even in "the true theologians [who] sought and fought against the roots and beginnings of error" (*Guide*, p. 317). Otherwise hate becomes evil itself, and it must be said that here Pound himself has erred at times, misguided as he was in his reforming zeal.

Yet if man's first aim is to live a full life, he will for ever try to make his love a full love, and that is achieved by desiring to know. "To improve [his] curiosity and not to fake,"[17] that is the road to love. On this journeying, in this sailing after knowledge, "what counts is the direction of the will" (*Impact*, p. 50), the desire for "the lifting up," to "raise the will" (*Impact*, p. 136). Once this "humanitas" has been attained, men will share in the divine vision, the crux of which is that

> things have roots and branches; affairs have scopes and
> beginnings,[18]

that, as the motto of *Jefferson and/or Mussolini* states,

> nothing is without efficient cause.

The divine does not, however, reveal itself if there is no reverence; the mysteries must be approached humbly; it demands total piety. Kung must be joined by Eleusis, as Civic order is nothing without religion. Only when the Odes have been studied[19] and the rites performed can the vision be threefold:

ALTAR   CITY   ROSE.[20]

The City is based on the mysteries, and the order of the city must harmonize with the order above; and "above all this" there is,

---

[17]*Paris Review*, 28, 28.

[18]Ezra Pound, *Confucius: The Great Digest & Unwobbling Pivot* (Peter Owen, 1952).

[19]Meant are, of course, the poems in the *Shih Ching*, translated by Pound as *The Classic Anthology Defined by Confucius*. "Kung's insistence on the ODES," Pound holds, "lifts him above all occidental philosophers." Moreover: "...people need poetry; ... prose is NOT education but the outer courts of the same. Beyond its doors are the mysteries. Eleusis. Things not to be spoken save in secret." (*Guide*, pp. 127 & 144f.).

[20]This pattern was emphasized by Forrest Read (*Sewanee Review*, LXV, 400–419).

Pound asserts, "the substantiality of the soul, and the substantiality of the gods" (*Impact*, p. 66).

The less love is mixed with hate the nearer the soul is to the gods in the heaven of Light and Love, and the more it shares the divine vision, "the *forma*, the immortal *concetto*" (*Guide*, p. 152). However:

> So slow is the rose to open.
> A match flares in the eyes' hearth,
>   then darkness   (106:104).

You have this vision only

> For a flash,
>   for an hour,
> Then agony,
>   then an hour,
>   then agony   (92:80).

But although the vision is not continuous, the knowledge of its beauty

> . . . has carved the trace in the mind
> dove sta memoria   (76:35/485).

The "steel dust" of a lifetime's experience, for which "there is no substitute" (98:43), has nevertheless sprung "into order" (*Guide*, p. 152).

Yet the question which must worry literary criticism most is whether Pound's *Cantos* is really good poetry. As far as his major poems up to and including *Hugh Selwyn Mauberley* and his merits as one of the men who made twentieth-century verse possible are concerned, there is practically a consensus of opinion; as to the *Cantos* there is none so far. Of the critics who do not dismiss the *Cantos* from the start most have their lists of "flawless" Cantos, some of which have already established themselves as anthology pieces,[21] and despite Kenner's advocacy for the whole poem, critical opinion now tends to stress its unevenness.

It seems to me, however, that there is one kind of poetry in the *Cantos* in which Pound's mastery and intensity have, right through to the end of *Thrones* and to the fragments of the continuation already accessible, never slackened. I refer to the nature lyrics, which range from simple observation of natural phenomena to mythi-

---

[21]For such a list see George Dekker, *Sailing After Knowledge* (1963), p. 203.

cally heightened chants. The Morning, Noon, and Evening lyrics in Canto IV give us ample proof of this. The most conspicuous example is, however, Canto XLIX, what Kenner calls "the emotional still point of *The Cantos*,"[22] with the most exquisite opening line:

> For the seven lakes, and by no man these verses.

That these nature lyrics impress themselves on the mind more than most of the other verses of perfect cadence and phrasing is as it should be, for they embody that great guide for Pound: the natural process; and that Pound puts his warmest affection into them we may gather from these lines written in Pisa:

> the sage
> delighteth in water
> the humane man has amity with the hills   (83:107/564).

To the delight in water, one of the great early stimuli having been Homer's epithet "poluphloisboios" (V. *Personae*, p. 191 & 74:5/453), add his worship of the tensile light, and Pound's poetic nucleus is all there, as in this passage from Canto CXV:

> ubi amor
> ibi oculus
> ? to all men for an instant ?
> beati
> The sky leaded with elm boughs
> A blown husk that is finished
> but the light sings eternal
> a pale flare over marshes
> where the salt hay whispers to tide's change.[23]

Remembering the early Pound, one cannot but quote the opening line of Δώρία, because it most aptly brings out what we experience:

> Be in me as the eternal moods   (*Personae*, p. 80).

As the poet of such moods, full of affectionate identification with trees, hills, lakes—anything in the "green world" (V. 81:99/556)— the author of the *Cantos* has no rival.

On the whole, and notwithstanding all that now passes as failures, there certainly are in the *Cantos*, as Charles Norman says,

---

[22]Hugh Kenner, *The Poetry of Ezra Pound* (Faber and Faber, 1951), p. 326.

[23]Printed in *Agenda* (London), 3 (Dec.-Jan. 1963/4, 3). The version given in *Paris Review*, 28, 13, is without the first 5 lines quoted here.

"passages by the score [which] make one fall in love again with the English tongue."[24] Even now a great deal of it can be read "just for the tone" (Tate); that charm of a Catallus which was very early felt[25] is still there to be enjoyed. On the other hand, Pound himself is aware that "there's need of elaboration, of clarification . . . There is no doubt that the writing is too obscure as it stands."[26] He even said on the BBC that the idea would be to "tuck in all the foot-notes," and then heaved a long sigh. Pound is, however, not too worried about this himself, because it has become more important to him just to point out that there is "something decent in the universe" (95:107), and that:

> In short, the cosmos continues   (87:33),

than to write nothing but poetry acceptable by traditional literary standards. The Cosmos, he says,

>   . . . coheres all right
>   even if my notes do not cohere.[27]

A recent interview showed Pound to have sunk into a state of lethargy. He now confesses that a lot of what he did is wrong, and he speaks of great doubts.[28] This has led the popular press to rejoice and virtually to say: "Ah good, the old blighter is finally recant-ing!" Has Pound really been wrong about everything? We leave this question for all those to ponder who care, but quote Pound once more, saying about himself:

> Many errors,
>   a little rightness,
> to excuse his hell and my paradiso,

and:

> It is difficult to write a paradiso when all the superficial indications are that you ought to write an apocalypse.[29]

24Norman, p. 335.

25See the newspaper comment quoted by T. S. Eliot in *Ezra Pound: His Metric and Poetry* (New York, 1917), p. 23.

26*Paris Review*, 28, 49.

27From Canto 116 (*Paris Review*, 28, 16).

28See Grazia Livi, "Io So Di Non Sapere Nulla," *Epoca* (Milan, March 24, 1963), 90–93. For the echo in the press see *New York Herald Tribune* (Paris, March 23–24, 1963) and *Daily Express* (March 23, 1963).

29*Paris Review*, 28, 16 & 47.

Loisann Oakes

An Explication of "Canto LXXV" by Ezra Pound

Excellence endures and it is upon us to preserve it and present it, itself. Clark Emery in *Ideas into Action, a study of Pound's Cantos* suggests how "Canto LXXV" comments on this fact and on the need of the writer to give *the thing* as a whole and not simply to refer to it. In using this ideogrammic technique Pound averts "the dangers of divisiveness" and points up "the need for dissociations."[1] But Pound assumes a prior knowledge of each *thing* within the Canto on the part of the reader; and an understanding of "Canto LXXV" must begin with simple identifications.

Phlegethon, also called Pyriphlegethon, is the river of fire of Hades. It flows from Styx to Acheron.[2]

Gerhart Münch is a pianist of whom little is known other than his association with Ezra Pound. He participated in the concerts given in Rapallo during the middle nineteen thirties.[3]

Detrich Buxtehude (*ca.* 1637-1707) was a composer and organist living in Lübeck in what is now North Germany. He initiated the *Abendmusiken* concerts. During the middle nineteen thirties interest in Buxtehude was stimulated by the publication of several scholarly books and articles. The collected edition of his works had begun to be published in 1925.[4]

Klages (Charles Klage, ?-1850) was a guitarist, pianist and composer. He published variations and arrangements of symphonic works for piano.[5]

From Loisann Oakes, "An Explication of 'Canto LXXV' by Ezra Pound," *Wisconsin Studies in Contemporary Literature*, V (© 1964 by the Regents of the University of Wisconsin), pp. 105–9. Reprinted by permission of the publisher.

[1]Clark Emery, *Ideas into Action* (Coral Gables, 1958), p. 137.

[2]*Paulys Real-Encyclopädie de Classiche Allertumswissenschaft*, ed. by Wissowa, Kroll, Mittelhaus (Stuttgart, 1941).

[3]John Hamilton Edwards, *Annotated Index to the Cantos of Ezra Pound* (Berkeley, Cal., 1957).

[4]Donald Jay Grout, *A History of Western Music* (New York, 1960), pp. 336-337.

[5]F. J. Fetis, *Biographie des Musiciens* (Paris, 1884), Vol. V, p. 46.

Stammbuch of Sachs. A *Stammbuch* is a genealogical table of a family; for example, the family tree of Hans Sachs, the *Meister-singer,* or even the *Meistersänger* as a group,[6] or this might refer to the opera by Wagner, *Die Meistersinger.*

— *not of one bird but of many* refers to the following example of music. It is Gerhart Münch's transcription of Clement Janequin's four voice *chanson, Reveilles-vous* (Chant des Oiseaux), published in 1539. It was transcribed for lute by Francesco da Milano in the sixteenth century and then transcribed for violin and piano in the twentieth century. The music seen as part of "Canto LXXV" is a photograph of a copy of the music made by Olga Rudge, the violin-ist. She played it with Münch in Rapallo. Her initials with the date and place appear at the end of the manuscript in the photograph.[7] The line itself is a paraphrase of what Münch said on first playing the piece, "Not one bird but a lot of birds."[8]

As one can see above, the rhythm of the words corresponds to the rhythm of the music, stretching the rhythm a bit or condensing it here and there. Even the pitch of the words has the same shape as the melodic line. The exclamation point in line one tells the reader that his reading must be emphatic, so "-thon" is set to a quarter note and two eighth notes tied, thus drawing out the vowel sound.

---

[6]J. H. Edwards, *op. cit.*

[7]J. H. Edwards, letter to L. A. Oakes, May 23, 1961.

[8]E. Pound, "Janequin, Francesco da Milano," *Townsman Quarterly,* I (1938), 18.

The comma in line two shows that the phrase moves toward the two half notes of "Gerhart." Pound places the name alone on line three corresponding to the first use of the half note in the piece, that is, a stretch in time. Line four has a question mark; the music rises in pitch but continues on, therefore Pound starts line five with a word in lower case. In line five "in your" is written out, sung to two written out quarter notes set on different pitches. In line six "in yr/" cannot receive as much stress as "your" in the previous line. The dash shows a break in thought. The rhythm shifts in order to present the music.

Pound's interest in music has been stated and re-stated throughout his prose writing. "Poetry is a composition of words set to music. It must be read as music and not as poetry" (*Vers libre and Arnold Dolmetsch*). This interest culminated in his theory of the three parts of poetry. The first part, *melopoeia*, is rhythm, especially, but combined with sound which then intermingles and becomes unchangeable. "I believe in an ultimate and absolute rhythm as I believe in an absolute symbol or metaphor. . . . in perfect rhythm joined to the perfect word. . . the two-fold vision can be recorded. . . . music is . . . perfect rhythm. . . . the rhythm set in a line of poetry connotes its symphony. . . . the rhythm of any poetic line corresponds to emotion. . . ." (*Introduction to Cavalcanti Poems*) This belief he evolved during his studies of Provençal poets and their sung-poems. The second part of his poetic theory, *phanopoeia*, is the image that lives and moves when it is in juxtaposition with other images within a poem. "I mean the ideograph of admirable compound-of-qualities that make any work of art permanent" (*Antheil and the Treatise on Harmony*). "The undeniable tradition of metamorphosis teaches us that things do not always remain the same. They become other things by swift and unanalysable process" (*Arnold Dolmetsch*). This "idea in action" is a technique derived from his studies and translations of Chinese poems from Japanese translations and is called the ideogram. The third part of his theory, *logopoeia*, is the use of language and its devices to instigate "good" reading. Words carefully chosen bring up associations and ideas in the mind of the reader necessary for the understanding of the poem as a totality. "Style, the attainment of a style consists in so knowing words that one will communicate the various degrees and weights of importance which one wishes" (*Guide to Kulchur*).

Ezra Pound juxtaposes Greek literature with Renaissance, Baroque, and Classic musicians, all bound together by a "translator."

The choice seems logical when the linear rather than the vertical emphasis of these periods of music are considered. Ancient Greek poetry was performed with music and dance. Music was an integral part of the total effect. In his view that poetry is "words set to music," Pound restated the ancient view of a synthesis of the arts to create the total "affect" within the reader. "The charm of Mozart seems often to lie in a rare combination of notes which have musical structure, musical line, but which suggest, beyond these and simultaneously, dance steps and language" (*Antheil and the Treatise on Harmony*). In general, each work of the Baroque typified an "affection," that is, one emotion: joy, grief, horror. The contrast came between movements of a work rather than within the work itself. In the late Renaissance the descriptive use of music was used to an extreme. In madrigals, if the word "rise" appeared, the line of music ascended; if the word "pants" appeared, the musical line would be interrupted with frequent rests.

Pound puts *phanopoeia* to great use in the poem. Visually, the reader hears the musician juxtaposed against the fiery river, and the song of the birds. Within each word there arises other images. When Pound asks "Gerhart art thou come forth out of Phlegethon?" he could mean that Münch arrived in Rapallo from Nazi Germany of the early thirties. Or, writing this in Pisa after the war might provide a clue. The war is symbolized as fire, the fire which had swept over Europe. Again, fire is used as a catharsis; Münch is cleansed by his association with Pound and by his coaching in order to "re-create" music. He had come "over Lethe," "out of Phlegethon." Pound connects the previous "Canto LXXIV" with this Canto using the two rivers of Hades, of forgetfulness and of fire. Münch becomes a part of the past and the present of Pound, associated through Phlegethon to "we who have passed over Lethe" (Canto LXXIV).

Buxtehude and Klage were probably in Gerhart Münch's briefcase in the form of music. But Klage is not "Klages," in which form Pound used the word. In German *Klages* is the genitive of *Klage* and would mean "of the lament" or "of the accusation." Looking further in the German dictionary you can find: *Buxe* (trousers), *Hudel* (rag or tatter), *Stammbuch* (album, genealogical register), *Sache* (thing), and *Saches* (of the thing). Gerhart had come out of Nazi Germany, because of an accusation, with his clothes in shreds and an album of things in his luggage. A far-fetched image, and yet, is it? All are things that carry on the unbroken line of German creativity beginning definitely with the time of Hans Sachs.

The choice of words dovetails *logopoeia* with *phanopoeia*. Pound has obviously chosen his words carefully. The sounds of the words play an important part. In the beginning Pound emphasizes the unvoiced "th": Phlege*th*on, for*th*; the voiced "th": *th*ou, wi*th*; and then he leads into the unvoiced "s" and the voiced "z": Bu*x*tehude, Klage*s*, *s*atchel, Sach*s*. The middle and back vowels "a" and "u": lead to one front vowel "i": man*y*. Rhythm is established by the repetition of "out of Phlegethon." ". . . focus mind on rhythm, intensely, to become more aware of that given form, and more sensitive to all other forms, rhythms, defined planes, or masses" (*Antheil and the Treatise on Harmony*).

Repetition, when used as variation, is included as a form of composition. Buxtehude is well known for his chorale variations. He would take a chorale tune, and each stanza of the chorale would serve in turn as a basis for elaboration by voices and instruments. Klage, as an arranger of music for the piano, was in another sense a person who dealt in repetitions.

The *logopoeia* appears when the variations of Buxtehude are associated with those of Klage and with those of the *chanson*. Within the *chanson* itself there is imitation and reiteration. It seems to conjure up concentric circles which can be viewed from within moving out or from without moving in. "Münch has an equal right, and is equally laudable in settling the same eternal beauty in the fiddle. If the piano obscures the fiddle, I have a perfect right to HEAR Janequin's intervals, his melodic conjunction from the violin solo. . . ." (*Guide to Kulchur*)

The ideogram is the music itself, an example of recreation. It is one piece from which we remember many pieces, "not of one bird but of many." The work recalls those who performed it, those who had previously varied it, and those who heard it during these many metamorphoses. "Janequin's concept takes a third life in our time, for catgut of patent silver, its first was choral, its second on the wires of Francesco Milano's lute. And its ancestry I think goes back to Arnaut Daniel and to God knows what 'hidden antiquity' " (*Guide to Kulchur*). It also projects our mind to future attempts of variation and of reconstruction of past art. "The two pages of Janequin are there, indestructible. . . . The ideogram of real composition is in Münch two pages, which belong to no man. . . . The gist, the pith, the unbreakable fact is there in the two pages of violin part. . . . Objectivity? The presentation in one art of what cannot be given in any other. It can imply, it can concentrate into itself any amount of implication, and does 'epitomize' etc. . . . The bed rock

in any art is composed of such solids. You could construct music
again from a few dozen such proofs of invention" ("Janequin, Francesco da Milano," *Townsman Quarterly*).

George Dekker

[Time and Tradition in
The Cantos]

1. The Pisan Sequence

> Where memory liveth,
>   it takes its state
> Formed like a diafan from light on shade
> Which shadow cometh of Mars and remaineth
> Created, having a name sensate,
> Custom of the soul,
>   will from the heart;
> Cometh from a seen form which being understood
> Taketh locus and remaining in the intellect possible

Pound's claim to greatness may well be held to rest with *The
Pisan Cantos*. They are the quintessentially Poundian achievement,
surely one of the most impure pieces of poetry ever written. If criticism were a matter of distinguishing models for young poets (as
Pound usually assumes) then a critic might reasonably put the sequence on his Index. Yet, for my own part, I find the sequence very
moving indeed, and the only part of the poem where Pound's characteristic obscurity does not annoy me very much. But it must be
owned that these cantos are extremely obscure, incredibly miscel-
laneous, and, so far as I can tell, not organized according to any
clear design.[1]

From *The Cantos of Ezra Pound: A Critical Study* (New York: Barnes and
Noble, 1963), pp. 188-204. Also entitled *Sailing After Knowledge: The Cantos
of Ezra Pound* (London: Routledge and Kegan Paul, 1963). Reprinted by
permission of the publishers.
[1]However, see Mr. Emery's discussion of *The Pisan Cantos* in *Ideas into Action*. His notes on the sequence are quite detailed and helpful.

From one point of view, however, all that is essential is that the reader of *The Pisan Cantos* know who Pound is, where he is, and when it is. For if the sequence holds together at all, it does so because it is fundamentally a dramatic monologue, because at last Odysseus-Pound has been trapped in the tragic plot of history, and because he has nothing but his own past and present to make poetry out of. This in itself is a formal advantage when he denies himself elsewhere in the poem except on rare occasions. Obscurity as such, if never a virtue, is much less crippling within a dramatic context. That the situation is potentially dramatic (whatever we may think of Pound for being in it) can hardly be denied. Perhaps following Shelley's argument in the *Defence of Poetry*, Pound once remarked of the Pedro-Ignez da Castro episode retold in Canto XXX, that 'the great poem, "Ignez da Castro", was written in deeds by King Pedro. No poem can have such force as has the simplest narration of the events themselves'.[2] It seems clear to me that Pound did fall into such a situation, and further that he was well aware of it.

Besides offering him a dramatic situation, his predicament allowed him to dramatize to artistic effect what seems to me the chief defect in his poetic gift — a split between the artist and the man, which does not exist when he acts or writes as a man of letters (as in *Propertius* and *Mauberley*), which is healed in several of the 'Fifth Decad of Cantos' and perhaps in the Chinese history cantos, but which crops up frequently and disruptively elsewhere. In the Pisan sequence Pound capitalizes this defect as only a very fine artist could. Besides the great hoard of esoteric objects stored up in his memory, which bejewel his reverie, there are in this sequence those glimpses of the D.T.C. compound and its inmates which reveal Pound responding as a human being, as much at ease as could be expected. These two levels, of the timeless and the temporal, the esoteric and the familiar, are united in the great and not so great artists and poets whom Pound has known and remembered here:

> Lordly men are to earth o'ergiven
> these the companions:

[2]*Spirit of Romance*, p. 230. An interesting confirmation of Pound's claim can be found in an aside by Professor W. J. Entwistle to the effect that, had the ballad then flourished in Portugal, the death of Ignez would certainly have been a likely theme (*European Balladry* [Oxford, 1939], p. 191). Shelley and Pound seem to me obviously right, whether our critical theory can account for it or not. Pound's awareness of such matters is also evidenced by his heroic record of the flight of the transatlantic pilot in Canto XXVIII, pp. 144–5: this, too, might have been celebrated in a ballad if the technology which made the flight possible had not wiped out balladry.

        Fordie that wrote of giants
        and William who dreamed of nobility
        and Jim the comedian singing:
        'Blarrney castle me darlin'
        you're nothing now but a StOWne'
                        (Canto LXXIV, p. 459)

A good example of Pound's ability to make poetry out of the D.T.C.
compound is the following passage (Pound has been observing a
wasp build a nest):

    It comes over me that Mr. Walls must be a ten-strike
    with the signorinas
    and in the warmth after chill sunrise
    an infant, green as new grass,
    has stuck its head or tip
    out of Madame La Vespa's bottle
    mint springs up again
                in spite of Jones' rodents
    as had the clover by the gorilla cage
            with a four-leaf

    When the mind swings by a grass-blade
        an ant's forefoot shall save you
    the clover leaf smells and tastes as its flower

        The infant has descended,
        from mud on the tent roof to Tellus,
    like to like colour he goes amid grass-blades
            greeting them that dwell under XTHONOS XΘONOΣ
    OI XΘONIOI; to carry our news
        εἰς χθονίους   to them that dwell under the earth
    begotten of air, that shall sing in the bower
        of Kore,   περσεφόνεια
    and have speech with Tiresias, Thebae
                        (Canto LXXXIII, p. 568)

This immediacy of perception is fairly frequent in *The Pisan Cantos,* as it is not in other parts of his work. Pound's imagination has
always been visual and, in its way, distinguished; but the perception
here is as fresh as the best of Hemingway's, yet better because it has
humour and learning to complement it. The element of poetic fan-
tasy is not new in Pound's work, but it is stronger in the Pisan
sequence (as it is again, notably, in Canto 91). The bowling alley
image which Pound uses to sum up Mr. Walls's virile powers is
(1) an accurate recollection of one of the mating grounds of urban

America; (2) a friendly criticism of the degree of consciousness and chastity which prevails there; (3) a striking variation on the image of the sperm driving into the egg. Whether it does not also record Mr. Walls's promiscuous masculine fantasies can be decided by each reader, according to his judgment of Pound's powers of insight and compression.

Such exhibits of a peculiarly Poundian excellence could be multiplied by anybody undertaking a full defence of the Pisan sequence, and many exhibits of a less admirable character could be produced by anybody undertaking an attack. What matters, however, is whether the 'good things' are nuggets glowing in a cave, illuminated by the lamp of an occasional lost critic, or whether the sequence as a whole is luminous, so that the exact contour of nearly every phrase and exact colour of nearly every word are immediately apparent. To my mind the latter is true, but I cannot enter here upon the kind of discussion required to defend this judgment.

What must be emphasized, however, is the sheer range of diction which Pound manages in these cantos. He is as much at ease with this:

> (O Mercury god of thieves, your caduceus
> is now used by the american army
>   as witness this packing case)
> Born with Buddha's eye south of Mason and Dixon
>   (Canto LXXVII)

as he is with this:

> Tudor indeed is gone and every rose,
> Blood-red, blanch-white that in the sunset glows
> Cries: 'Blood,   Blood,   Blood!' against the gothic stone
> Of England, as the Howard or Boleyn knows.
>   (Canto LXXX)

The one may be 'Poetry' and the other 'prose', but there is the same grip on language, no fondling of exotic words: because at this late stage in *The Cantos*, and in his career, Pound is as much at ease with 'Mercury god of thieves' as he is with the negro prisoner who stole the packing case for him to use as a desk. In the stanza modelled on Fitzgerald's *Rubaiyat*, the first line is so contrived that 'every rose' may be the subject of an implied predicate 'is gone' or, as it turns out, of 'Cries'. Ambiguous syntax of this kind is quite the opposite of decadence or even of decadence illustrated and by im-

plication criticized, as in *Gerontion* and *The Waste Land*. For this
ambiguity illustrates not merely the motion of the mind as it first
muses upon a 'rose' that is merely conventional, unvisualized, and
then upon a rose which, as it gathers concreteness, gathers also
those historical and symbolical properties which draw the imagination back in time, to the England which Pound is to celebrate in
Canto 91; but it illustrates, as well, the power of syntax to renew
itself and invigorate poetry. There is a great deal more than mere
craftsmanship involved in such poetry; but such poetry does not
come into being without 'mere craftsmanship'.

Indeed, the long passage dealing with England, from which this
stanza is extracted, may be taken as a text to illustrate the indivis-
ible relationship between Pound's peculiar use of language and his,
I should say, not at all peculiar way of recalling and valuing the
past. The peculiarity and unrepeatableness of the achievement is,
however, something that should be stressed: *The Pisan Cantos*
are as odd as *Tristram Shandy*. I give part of the passage immediately preceding the stanza discussed above.

> and for that Christmas at Maurie Hewlett's
> Going out from Southampton
> they passed the car by the dozen
>   who would not have shown weight on a scale
>   riding, riding
>   for Noel the green holly
>   Noel, Noel, the green holly
>   A dark night for the holly
>
> That would have been Salisbury plain, and I have not
>   thought of
>   the Lady Anne for this twelve years
>   Nor of Le Portel
> How tiny the panelled room where they stabbed him
>   In her lap, almost, La Stuarda
>   Si tuit li dolh ehl planh el marrimen
>   for the leopards and broom plants

There is no point in pretending that all of this would be intelligible
to Pound's English reader, much less to his American reader. It
moves, as reverie does move, by association; but it is the carefully
edited reverie of a full mind, and the accidental element in the association, though to some extent real, is also a carefully preserved
illusion. It is real to the extent that Hewlett was a romancer and

poetical historian of England whom Pound knew and liked, and to
the extent that he apparently visited the places mentioned. That
Pound knew Hewlett and visited these places does not, in itself,
matter to his reader, except in so far as they stand for something
he understands or can understand. Whether Pound can expect his
reader to have a necessary superficial acquaintance with Hewlett's
work is a question which I can't answer; and it may be that the passage is sufficiently clear without that acquaintance. In any case,
Pound did know Hewlett and apparently believed that he embodied
peculiarly English virtues and that the English past was still alive
in him. And what Pound is implying here and throughout *The Pisan
Cantos* is that, yes, it matters very much to him that he knew Hewlett and that he took these journeys; for in so far as the English past
is alive and meaningful to him, it is so because of these concrete associations, with man and rooms and journeys; with the Christmas
holly in which tree spirits took refuge before the Christian era;
with 'the leopards and broom plants' which were the heraldic devices of Richard Cœur-de-Lion and the Plantagenets; and with a
line from Bertrans de Born's 'Planh' for the Young English King,
Prince Henry Plantagenet.[3]

Then begins the stanza in which Pound recalls the English roses
to life, roses which are the counterparts of the leopards and broom
plants. It is true that he does not develop the earlier images fully,
yet it would be foolish to assert that 'leopards' = Richard. The heraldic device recalls Richard in a special way, via the trappings and
pageantry of mediaeval chivalry. There are of course many sides to
Richard, among them his cruelty and bankrupting ambition and
preference for the climate and language of southern France; and
young Prince Henry Plantagenet was, besides a gallant knight and
patron of troubadours like Bertrans, a wastrel and a renegade
against his father, the king who adopted broom plants as his device
and who brought about the martyrdom of Thomas, etc. Pound's references, then, have a specific weight and value, as important for
what they exclude as for what they include. And there can be no

[3]This Pound once translated, not very closely, yet beautifully:
  If all the grief and woe and bitterness,
  All dolour, ill and every evil chance
  That ever came upon this grieving world
  Were set together they would seem but light
  Against the death of the young English King.
  Worth lieth riven and Youth dolorous,
  The world o'ershadowed, soiled and overcast,
  Void of all joy and full of ire and sadness.

objection if Pound wishes (as most of us do) to recall the chivalric
Richard, generous and talented and courageous; for in the Pisan
Cantos he is not (or only rarely) trying to 'prove' this or to 'expose'
that or even to instruct us very much — though the sequence is certainly instructive.

Behind this procession of anecdotes and heraldic devices and
meticulously rendered scenes from the D.T.C. compound, there lies
the conception expressed in Canto XXXVI:

> Where memory liveth,
>   it takes its state
> Formed like a diafan from light on shade
>
> Which shadow cometh of Mars and remaineth
> Created, having a name sensate
> Custom of the soul,
>   will from the heart;
>
> Coming from a seen form which being understood
> Taketh locus and remaining in the intellect possible

In Pound's case it is true that 'memory liveth', and the many anecdotes, places, and sayings recorded in the Pisan sequence 'cometh
from a seen form which being understood/Taketh locus and remain-
ing in the intellect possible'. The following example of this process
is also a gentle parody of it:

> Well, Campari is gone since that day
>   with Dieudonné and with Voisin
> and Gaudier's eye on the telluric mass of Miss Lowell
>   (Canto LXXVII)

Like Pound, Gaudier brings a professional eye to bear on the objects
around him, storing the significant details away for future use. (In
context the humour is even greater, for Pound cuts abruptly from
'the telluric mass of Miss Lowell' to ' "the mind of Plato ... or that
of Bacon" ' — p. 498.)

The phrase 'a seen form which being understood' underscores the
necessity of actual personal experience accompanied by a perception of its significance. (Pound is fond of Spinoza's 'the intellectual
love of a thing consists in the understanding of its perfections'.)[4]
This approach is based, of course, on the premise that the observer
has had access to significant individuals, events, and works of art

---

[4]Quoted by Pound in *Literary Essays*, pp. 71, 184, and 204.

— and this Pound certainly has had. Among these many sought-after contacts, none was more important than his friendship with Gaudier-Brzeska. And ultimately the great elegy which *The Pisan Cantos* comprise, an elegy for all that Pound knew and loved before World War II, is based on his grief and reflections over the death of Gaudier in World War I. Gaudier's death is recorded very modestly in Canto XVI:

> And Henri Gaudier went to it,
> and they killed him,
> and killed a good deal of sculpture.

Modest this is, but Pound's grief and outrage are recorded elsewhere (in his *Gaudier-Brzeska* particularly, and, more impersonally, in Poems IV and V of *Mauberley*[5]). How they 'killed a good deal of sculpture' is, generally speaking, obvious enough; but Pound has something more specific in mind:

> 'as the sculptor sees the form in the air
> before he sets hand to mallet,
> 'and as he sees the in, and the through,
> the four sides
> (Canto XXV)

Because of the nature of his medium (if he carves or chisels), he simply must 'see the form in the air/before he sets hand to mallet', because there is no turning back once he begins to sculpt. It is, then, peculiarly true of a sculptor like Gaudier that the work is actually in existence before it receives its concrete embodiment; and from this point of view the Germans did literally 'kill a good deal of sculpture' as well as an enormous potential. The development of this idea can be followed in these images, the first from Canto XXXVI and the second from the Pisan sequence:

> Yet shall ye see of him That he is most often
> With folk who deserve him
> And his strange quality sets sighs to move
> Willing man look into that forméd trace in his mind
>
> nothing matters but the quality
> of the affection—
> in the end—that has carved the trace in the mind
> dove sta memoria

[5]Echoes of the ideas and phrasing of Poems IV and V can be found in *Gaudier-Brzeska* (new ed., 1961), pp. 17, 54, 110.

When he set out on *The Cantos* Pound was concerned chiefly with
wasted potential, the sculptor with the form in the mind, which was
destroyed with the sculptor; in *The Pisan Cantos* he is on this side
of World War II, concerned with the passing away of men and
things which exist now only in the mind, and there only because he
had studied them with affection and taken careful mental note of
them. But the cost of war to civilization in general

> is measured by the *to whom* it happens
> and to what, and if to a work of art
> then to all who have seen and who will not
> (Canto LXXVI)

All of these ideas are brought together in the famous passage
which closes Canto LXXXI:

> What thou lovest well remains,
>   the rest is dross
> What thou lov'st well shall not be reft from thee
> What thou lov'st well is thy true heritage
>
> Whose world, or mine or theirs
>   or is it of none?
> First came the seen, then thus the palpable
>   Elysium, though it were in the halls of hell,

The 'halls of hell' are of course the places where Odysseus-Pound
has gone to see Tiresias, and there is more than one Elysian Field:

> Romains, Vildrac, and Chennevière and the rest of
>   them
> before the world was given over to wars
> Quand vous serez bien vielle
>   remember that I have remembered,
>   (Canto LXXX)

Usually the great passage of general statement at the end of Canto
LXXXI is anthologized by itself, apart from the many particular
recollections which it subsumes. This is perhaps the inevitable fate
of a poetry which enshrines so many 'significant details', whose significance is not always generally recognized or comprehended. But
it is by the peculiar, individual qualities of men and things that
Pound remembers them; and it is the essence of his poetic principles
and methods that he should set these particulars down as his testimony that he has 'seen' and 'understood' Yeats or Joyce or whom-
ever — quite the opposite of:

> and Uncle William dawdling around Notre Dame
> in search of whatever
>   paused to admire the symbol
> with Notre Dame standing inside it
>   (Canto LXXXIII)

It is a modest bit of practical criticism, of the Yeats whose defect of interest in the thing itself led sometimes to embarrassing exaggeration ('On the Death of Major Robert Gregory'), but, under correction, to a mighty transformation ('Easter 1916'). Pound's style rarely transforms, nor is it calculated to. It is perhaps only in *The Pisan Cantos* that his translator's ethic really bears fruit.

For in that sequence, where he is OY TIΣ, he might well state as his first principle, 'Amo ergo sum, and in just that proportion' (Canto LXXX). He *is* only in so far as the things and men he loves define his being. They do not exist because of him. But, nevertheless, in the midst of death and destruction, it is Pound's memory and art that preserve the contour and quiddity of the things he loved.

2. Cantos 85–109

The Rock-Drill Cantos (1955) and *Thrones* (1959) bring the poem to within eleven cantos of the end. The main objective of these twenty-four cantos, and presumably of the cantos which will follow, is to enunciate the timeless principles upon which civilizations are built. This is not to say that Pound abandons his historical researches or that splendid lyrical passages are lacking; yet the pedagogical function of both sequences, whatever the subject or style of an individual canto, is far more explicit than before. Unfortunately, however, to communicate the philosophical basis of *The Cantos*, Pound continues to use the extreme elipses and cryptic allusions which were appropriate (if often frustrating) in *The Pisan Cantos*. At one point in *Thrones* he openly abandons the attempt to communicate with any except his most devoted students:

> *If we never write anything save what is already understood, the field of understanding will never be extended. One demands the right, now and again, to write for a few people with special interests and whose curiosity reaches into greater detail.*
>
> (Canto 96, p. 11)

This, it should be clear, is Cavalcanti-Pound speaking; and here, in the very late cantos, we have Pound's arcanum. In Canto LIII (p. 283) he once wrote, 'Taught and the not taught. Kung and Eleusis/

to catechumen alone'. And now anybody who wishes to read Pound must become a catechumen.

What must be insisted now is that Cantos I–LXXXIV, however cryptic or deformed in other respects, do represent a serious attempt to communicate with more than 'a few people with special interests'. And even in the cantos under discussion Pound does not give up the attempt entirely: Canto 99, for instance, should be fairly accessible to the lay-reader:

> People have bodies
> > ergo they sow and reap,
> Soldiers also have bodies,
> > take care of the body as implement,
> It is useful,
> To shield you from floods and rascality.
> > > (pp. 57–8)

However, those who wish to gain wisdom will probably do well to look elsewhere, perhaps in the books from which Pound mined these cantos.[6] Even the cantos which have much or some beauty — i.e. 90–93 and 106 — are maddeningly cryptic, though I believe that it is possible to defend Pound's cryptic method in the case of some of these cantos, 91 especially, on the grounds that no other method would quite do the job. As for the rest, they do not seem to me to reward the close study which they require. Perhaps when the *Annotated Index* is supplemented to include the post-Pisan Cantos, they will seem less difficult and more rewarding.

But at present I think that the reader's attention had better be concentrated on Canto 91. A full-scale exegesis would be out of place here. At this point I merely wish to indicate how Pound's cryptic method actually functions poetically. Canto 91, it will be recalled, is concerned with the recurrence of certain values or artistic insights:

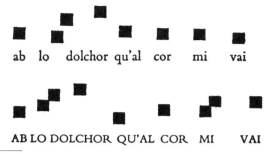

---

[6]Information about Pound's sources and a more sympathetic account of these cantos can be found in Mr. Emery's *Ideas into Action* and Mr. Kenner's 'Under the Larches of Paradise'. *Gnomon* (New York, 1958), pp. 280–96.

> that the body of light come forth
> > from the body of fire
> And that your eyes come to the surface
> > from the deep wherein they were sunken,
> Reina—for 300 years,
> > and now sunken
> That your eyes come forth from their caves
> > & light then
> > > as the holly-leaf
> > > qui laborat, orat
> Thus Undine came to the rock,
> > > by Circeo
> and the stone eyes again looking seaward

The musical annotation seems to recall the 'Song of the Birds' by Janequin, which Pound transcribed in Canto LXXV. According to Pound the song of the birds which was in Janequin's original has survived through many transcriptions for various instruments down the centuries.[7] On the strength of what follows in Canto 91, I should guess that Pound also believes that Janequin (or some unknown predecessor) had such inwardness with the singing of the birds that he discovered once and for all time how to register their music for reproduction by man-made instruments. The Provençal line appears to be Pound's own pastiche of lines taken from Bernart de Ventadorn and Guillem de Poitou.[8] A free translation of the relevant stanza in Guillem's song: 'With the sweetness of the springtime, the woods come into leaf and the birds sing, each in his own tongue, according to the style of the new song.' Bernart's song: 'When I see the lark move his wings joyously in a sun ray, then forgetting himself and letting himself fall, on account of the sweetness that comes into his heart.' Here indeed there is inwardness with nature and, more specifically, with the nature of birds. Nobody, I suppose, will deny the obscurity of these associations; but on the other hand, it is probably only necessary that the reader make the easy association of troubadour language with the idea of Eros as an instigation. If, however, one is fully aware of Pound's associations at the beginning of the canto, one is in a position to see how each cryptic phrase calls to mind a host of analogues from various centuries and various languages. Thus the 'Reina' of the following lines is not merely Elizabeth Tudor: she is the Diana who killed Actaeon; the Eleanor of Aquitaine to whom Bernart's song was directed across the En-

---

[7] Pound, *Guide to Kulchur*, p. 152.
[8] The Provençal lines are these: 'Ab lo dolchor del temps novel' and 'per la doussor c'al cor li vai' (*Anthology of Provençal Troubadours*, pp. 9 and 45). Pound's line: 'with the sweetness that comes into my heart'.

glish Channel; and the Virgin Mary in whose honour the troubadours sang after their courtly patrons were destroyed by the Albi-
gensian Crusade. A little farther on in the canto we encounter a
reference to Helen of Tyre, who is possibly a prototype of 'Our
Lady' of the troubadours, of the Christian hymn-makers, and of the
Tudor courtiers. These associations, if unavailable to most readers,
are perfectly valid; and it is precisely such associations, regarded as
recurrences of a permanently valuable concept, that are the real
subject of this canto. Though often beautiful and sharply denota-
tive in their own right, the actual words on the page exist chiefly
for the sake of suggesting and directing the line of association: thus
'Undine' suggests Hans Andersen's mermaid, Pound's Aphrodite
coming to shore, and Ibsen's Lady from the Sea — whose eyes were
as remarkable as those of Hérédia's Cléopatre or Pound's Miss
Tudor or Bernart's Eleanor.[9]

For Pound's purposes, it should be evident, the normal language
of poetry — language with the virtues of prose — would interfere
with the rapid interplay of association which is the chief action of
this canto. Such poetry can never be very widely understood or
appreciated, and it is to be hoped that other poets will not try to
follow in Pound's footsteps. However, Canto 91 seems to me the
most brilliant example of Pound's poetry of cryptic allusion and
the consummation of the poetic attitudes and techniques inspired
by Cavalcanti's *Canzone d'Amore*. There will always be a few people
(not necessarily Poundians) who will take the trouble to understand it, and in my opinion it is by far the most rewarding of the
cantos which follow the Pisan sequence.[10]

3. Cantos 110–?

Canto 120 is now supposed to be the last one, but it is apparent that
even the illusion of completion could be achieved only if Pound
were capable of a stupendous finale. Whether a poet in his late
seventies can be expected to enjoy another resurgence of poetic
powers — which have been ebbing since 1948 — seems highly unlikely, to say the least. However, it is probably wrong to suppose

---

[9]In the *canso* cited above, Bernart speaks of Eleanor's eyes as mirrors, which
suddenly metamorphose into the pool in which Narcissus drowned himself.
[10]Up to the italicized diatribe at the bottom of p. 73. For a tactful and in-
formed reading of this canto, see Donald Davie's ' "Forma" and "Concept" in
Ezra Pound's Cantos', *Irish Writing* (Autumn 1956), pp. 160–73.

that Pound intends a real conclusion: probably the poem will end with an exhortation (explicit or otherwise) to the faithful, urging them to continue the never-ending journey after knowledge which Odysseus-Pound got under way. In any event, I see little reason to suppose that the final cantos will alter my present conviction that the poem, as a poem, is a colossal failure. Perhaps its failure might have been less unquestionable if Pound had been willing to end with Canto 100 and if he had been able to suppress his urge to investigate such matters as the career of Thomas Hart Benton and the history of Byzantine coinage and interest rates. But in the end it is with Pound as it was with Ulysses: curiosity counts for more than good judgment, and so the poem itself — which it once seemed possible to end fairly happily — must follow the curve of Ulysses' fortunes.

Pound has suggested that when he finished *The Cantos* he might provide an 'Aquinas-map' for those who failed to see his design. I should certainly like to study such a map; for, as I have already admitted, I am able to discern only one 'plot' whose development has any formal significance — i.e. the major shifts in the relationship between time and the poetic endeavour — and this is so general as to be of very limited importance to the reader who is struggling in a sea of particulars. (Though I should insist that it is a matter of importance, and might have been of still greater importance if the post-Pisan Cantos had been more uniformly and intelligibly concerned with the timeless principles upon which civilizations are founded.) However, if Pound does produce his 'Aquinas-map', I do not see how it could really reveal any great formal design in *The Cantos*: if the design is so thoroughly buried in the particulars as to be invisible to all eyes save Pound's, then it hardly matters. Besides, the analogy with Dante's poem is pointless: useful as the accessory notes and diagrams are, one can perceive the major design of the *Commedia* without them; for the great system is firmly, if not always clearly, implicit in each of the details. Of *The Cantos* this is not and cannot be true.

Pound scholars will undoubtedly continue to write about the poem as though it were successful enough to be regarded as the great American epic, a poem as great as or greater than *Paradise Lost*. Though I do not share this view, I still feel that their researches into the meaning and form of the poem deserve respect and, in certain cases at least, encouragement. On the other hand, there are many readers who will continue to regard *The Cantos* as a poem which is entirely evil, sterile, or incomprehensible, or all three at the same time. And again, though I do not share this view, I agree that there is much in *The Cantos* that falls into these categories. Between these two camps there can be little understanding or sympathy; for while the one mistakes Pound's pure intentions for pure achievements, the other is hardly willing to touch the poem (or let others touch it) for fear of contamination. Of course *The Cantos* encourages such extreme reactions. It is a poem which invites its critic to regard himself as a chivalric defender of civilization, as the poem appears alternately in the guise of a dragon or a lady in distress. It is both, and the critic who thinks it is only a dragon or only a lady distressed by critical dragons, merely joins its author in tilting at windmills.

Therefore, I think that I should state my conclusions as firmly, clearly, and briefly as possible. Although I encourage readers, in justice to Pound, to examine the entire poem, yet I am satisfied that certain cantos are a great deal better than others and that these should be isolated for special attention. The best seem to me Cantos I, II, XVII, part of XXX, XLV, XLVII, XLIX, part of LI, and part of 91. The Pisan sequence must, I think, be taken as a whole, though there are of course several passages which make handsome anthology pieces. Other cantos of merit which are important for understanding the poem are Cantos III, IV, VII, XIII, XXXVI, and 90. To search out the beautiful fragments or passages in other cantos is not a waste of time by any means. But it seems to me vastly more important to isolate the cantos or parts of cantos which are fairly complete poetic wholes: for the best of these will survive; they are among the greatest poetic achievements of this century.

Though certainly very high, Pound's place among modern poets can hardly be fixed during his own life-time or for many years to come. Probably Yeats's brilliant evaluation of Pound, in its entirety, is the best short statement on the subject that we shall ever get; but here it is sufficient to quote only a part: 'When I consider his work as a whole I find more style than form; at moments more style, more deliberate nobility and the means to convey it than any contemporary poet known to me . . .'[11] I am not quite sure what reservation, if any, is implied in 'deliberate'; but 'deliberate nobility' is undoubtedly the right characterization of Pound's best work:

---

[11] Yeats, *Oxford Book of Modern Verse* (1936), pp. xxiii–xxvi.

> Rathe to destroy, niggard in charity,
> Pull down thy vanity,
>> I say pull down.

> But to have done instead of not doing
>> this is not vanity
> To have, with decency, knocked
> That a Blunt should open
>> To have gathered from the air a live tradition
> or from a fine old eye the unconquered flame
> This is not vanity.
>> Here error is all in the not done,
> all in the diffidence that faltered.

I have seen this described somewhere as (in the modern sense) an apology, much as those with little wit or honesty mention, in passing, *Mauberley* as Pound's confession of literary failure. Since the 'fine old eye' with 'the unconquered flame' perhaps belongs to Yeats, there may be some point in hearing what he has to say about the sort of critics with whom Pound has been commonly plagued, who have commented on his work with more self-righteous snickering than his abundant folly ever deserved, with but cautious recognition of his sometimes great achievements, and with utterly mean and incurious contempt for his titanic, if often misguided, effort:

> Come let us mock at the great
> That had such burdens on the mind
> And toiled so hard and late
> To leave some monument behind,
> Nor thought of the levelling wind.

But there is no reason to quote the rest of this great passage from 'Nineteen Hundred and Nineteen', at the end of which Yeats turns on the mockers themselves. It is the work of a greater poet than Pound, well remembered in the Pisan Cantos, as are so many of the great and fanatic figures of Pound's era.

William Cookson

Some Notes on *Rock-Drill* and *Thrones*

"The essential thing in a poet is that he builds us his world" Pound wrote in 1915. The world Pound has built in *The Cantos* mirrors, in a way which is unique, the state of the life of the mind of Europe, including America, in the twentieth century. There are many other sides to the poem (Mr Pound's interests extend far beyond Europe) but at its core *The Cantos* is a great visionary poem of European civilization written at a time when that civilization is in danger of falling apart.

> The scientists are in terror
> and the European mind stops (Canto 115)

It represents the effort of a lifetime to discriminate, hold together in the mind and bring to some sort of order the best elements of Europe's past. It is rooted in the two major poems of the Occident, *The Odyssey* and *The Divine Comedy* but it is never literary in a bad sense — Mr Pound has lived and suffered his subject matter directly. In these notes I intend to deal with the later Cantos, that is the two collections following the Pisans.

Surprise, as Eliot said, is one of the essential qualities in poetry. It is hard to think of a greater surprise in literature than the change in tone from the Adams Cantos to the first line in the Pisans: "The enormous tragedy of the dream in the peasant's bent shoulders". At Pisa the poet suffered the wreck of the Europe he loved, in actuality, which gives his vision a new depth. I think of King Lear, or the 'compound ghost' in *Little Gidding* who says "So I find words I never thought to speak". As a record of suffering, exposure to the elements and deepened understanding and serenity, "in the drenched tent there is quiet / sered eyes are at rest", there is little in the poetry of any language, with which to compare these great pages. I am thinking of the whole Pisan sequence, but in particular of the tranquility and *hilaritas* of the rain bright dawn in Canto 83,

Reprinted from *Agenda* (London), IV (October-November 1965), 30-37, by permission of the author and *Agenda*.

> there is no base seen under Taishan
> but the brightness of *'udor*
> the poplar tips float in brightness
> only the stockade posts stand
>
> And now the ants seem to stagger
> as the dawn sun has trapped their shadows, . . .

That was 1945. It was probably not until 1952 or 1953 that Pound started working on *The Cantos* again. *Section: Rock-Drill* was published in Italy in 1955.

It can be divided into two parts: 85–89 are historical, didactic; 90–95 is an immense lyric, "above civic order, L'AMOR", showing a kind of beauty that has not been present in English since medieval times and was only there in flashes then. These two parts animate each other, it is consequently impossible to understand one without the other; 85–89 provide an historical basis for 90–95. They are different sides of the same reality.

Pound came to a number of historical and economic conclusions after much research during the thirties and forties which were mostly embodied in a series of pamphlets written in Italian and now available in English translation in *Impact* (Regnery). The historical Cantos in the first half of *Rock-Drill* are very largely constructed (by what Pound was calling as early as 1911 "the method of luminous detail" . . . "certain facts give one a sudden insight into circumjacent conditions, into their causes their effects, into sequence and law") from material that will be found dealt with at greater length in *Impact*. This, and the *Guide to Kulchur*, are the essential companion volumes. It is, of course, impossible to enumerate the themes of Cantos 85–89 but they deal chiefly with what Mr Pound has called, "the two forces in history: one that divides, shatters and kills, and one that contemplates the unity of the mystery" which is best summed up by the phrase (Canto 86):

> Bellum cano perenne . . .
> between the usurer and
> any man who wants to do a good job

followed by Pound's definition of usury:

> without regard to production —
> a charge
> for the use of money or credit.

There is a new precision in the writing and these cantos do much
to clarify earlier parts of the poem that had seemed obscure. For
example, the account of Van Buren and the Bank War is seen in
the light of Thomas Hart Benton's great speech against the renewal
of the U.S. Bank Charter here summarized in Canto 88.

As T.S. Eliot pointed out in his essay on Dante, we have lost the
habit of seeing things in a visionary way. Cantos 90–95 do much to
restore this "lost kind of experience". No medieval visionary poetry
in English can compare with these sections of Mr Pound's poem —
we should have to look at Dante for anything finer.

> 'And if I see her not,
>   no sight is worth the beauty of my thought.'
> Then knelt with the sphere of crystal
> That she should touch with her hands,
>   Coeli Regina,
> The four altars at the four coigns of that place,
> But in the great love, bewildered
>   farfalla in tempesta
> under rain in the dark:
>   many wings fragile
> Nymphalidae, basilarch, and lycaena,
> Ausonides, euchloe, and erynnis
> And from far
>   il tremolar della marina

These six cantos, by a constant interaction between what is living
in the classical and medieval words, probably cohere in a way in
which intentionally earlier portions of the poem did not and this is
because they grow out of the highest use of the intellect, "contemplation" as defined by the twelfth century theologian Richard of
St. Victor in *Benjamin Major*. Beginning with Canto 90 we are in
what Mr Pound once called "the radiant world where one thought
cuts through another with clean edge, a world of moving energies
... magnetisms that take form, that are seen, or that border the
visible, the matter of Dante's *Paradiso*, the glass under water, the
form that seems a form seen in a mirror, these realities perceptible
to the sense, interacting ..." or, in the words of Richardus: "contemplation, guided by a ray of vision, sheds light over numberless
things." Thus enumerable themes are formed in the mind "to remain there, resurgent": the sea caves out of whose green depths
rise the eyes of Aphrodite, "manifest and not abstract"; the holly
leaf that St. Hilary may have looked at; the place where the light

was "almost solid"; first the crystal river and then the deep sapphire over which the Princess Ra-Set voyages, which is the same as that of the blue serpent that "glides from the rock pool"; the fountain of Castalia; the invocation to Diana (compare Canto 30); Odysseus who moves through Canto 94 in the form of Apollonius of Tyana, and thus the raising of the spirits of the dead, now with incense and myrrh: "It was not by ditch-digging and sheep's guts"; the great concourse of beasts before the altar in Canto 90: "and where was nothing now is furry assemblage" (note how the heaviness of the word "assemblage" seems to bring them physically before us); — these are a few of themes that, taking light from each other, build Mr. Pound's Paradise and, by the birth of Venus, Dea Libertatis, "crystal waves weaving together toward the great healing" help to give form to the whole poem.

These Cantos are so packed and their patterns of thought so complex that they will bear innumerable rereadings. Perhaps one aspect the academic commentators are apt to forget is their humour and closely allied to this, their use of the anecdotal quotation, something never employed in poetry before, or as Ub said:

> "ten to charge a nest of machine guns
> for one who will put his name on a chit."

The constant variation of speed and tone, the sense of a live man talking prevents any possibility of boredom — Pound in the later Cantos, has evolved a form that is ideally suited to the writing of a long poem. One canto will range from an aphorism like the above, to the sustained lyricism with its slow rhythm of the prayer beginning:

> The autumn leaves blow from my hand,
> agitante calescemus . . .
> and the wind cools toward autumn
> Lux in diafana,
> Creatrix,
> oro.

to the magical:

> Au bois dormant,
> not yet . . . ! Not yet!
> do not awaken.
> The trees sleep, and the stags, and the grass;
> The boughs sleep unmoving.

There is never any incongruity and whole worlds of experience are contained in each line, or half line. To quote a famous passage from Keats, Pound never "lets go an isolated verisimilitude caught from the Penetralium of Mystery" — as he says in Canto 93 from which these three quotations come: "There must be incognita." The political and economic cantos are the sort of poetry that "has a palpable design upon us" (and they sometimes pall in consequence) but the finest sections of *Rock-Drill* are entirely without faults of this kind.

Mr. Pound had some interesting things to say about *Thrones* in an interview in the *Paris Review* (Summer 1962). "Rock-Drill was intended to imply the necessary resistance in getting a certain main thesis across — hammering. I was not following the three divisions of the *Divine Comedy* exactly. One can't follow the Dantescan cosmos in an age of experiment. But I have made the division between people dominated by emotion, people struggling upwards, and those who have some part of the divine vision. The thrones in Dantes' *Paradiso* are for the spirits of the people who have been responsible for good government. The thrones in the *Cantos* are an attempt to move out from egoism and to establish some definition of an order possible or at any rate conceivable on earth. One is held up by the low percentage of reason which seems to operate in human affairs. *Thrones* concerns the states of mind of people responsible for something more than their personal conduct". Another quotation also seems useful in this context, from *Impact*, "History is recorded in monuments, *that* is why they get destroyed." *Thrones* is one of the most solid historical achievements of the *Cantos*. While illuminating the earlier parts of the poem it is a coherent structure in itself resting upon three monuments to justice and good government: the Eparchikon Biblion (the Byzantine Eparch's Edict), Iong Ching's commentary on his father's Sheng U (Sacred Edict) and the Institutes of Sir Edward Coke.

Canto 96 starts with the shipwrecked Odysseus, who has been saved from drowning, as recounted at the end of *Rock-Drill* by the sea nymph Leucothoe's veil which enables him to reach Phaeacia, seeing her disappear in the waves "and the wave concealed her / dark mass of great water." Canto 96 goes on "that should bear him through these diafana" with some of the most detailed historical analysis Mr Pound has written introducing us to the Eparch's Edict via much later Roman and Byzantine history. This is the first time that Byzantine Civilization is treated in the poem — "Constantinople" said Wynham, "our star". The whole Canto despite its obscure subject matter is one of the most lucid and readable in the poem, but, as it depends for its effect on the slow accumulation of individual facts, it is impossible to substantiate this statement here. It also contains a record of the war which Justinian II waged agaist Abdel Melik for striking and issuing 'gold coins without the Imperial stamp or authority' illustrating that the nature of kingship and sovereignty inheres in the prerogative over coinage. The documents to which the poem introduces us are always interesting in their own right.

The first half of Canto 97 is based largely on the work of the nineteenth century American historian Alexander Del Mar dealing with the ratio between gold and silver in Imperial Rome and the Orient and contains the memorable line: "When kings quit, the bankers began again." Some of it is very obscure. The second half gradually moves into lyricism and is full of subtlety of intonation exactly conveyed:

> 'As THAT!' said Ungaro,
> 'It is just as hard as that'
> (jabbing a steel cube with his pencil butt
> and speaking of mind as resistant)

In these late cantos Mr. Pound has found a form that can weave the lyrical, the factual and the didactic into a single texture — in consequence there are none of the dry stretches that we get in earlier parts of the poem.

Canto 99 "a condensation or emphasis on the Emperor Iong Ching's commentary on his father's Sacred Edict" rhymes with Canto 85 that deals with the pre-Confucian Shu, or history classic and taken with this and Canto 61 (the last China Canto that is also about Iong Ching) gives some idea how long the Confucian code remained vital. It is a hymn to good government and has a beauty that can be compared with the serenity, "That his ray come to point in this quiet", of the *Classic Anthology* translated a few years earlier.

> The sages of Han had a saying:
> Manners are from earth and from water
> They arise out of hills and streams
> The spirit of air is of the country
> Men's manners cannot be one
> (same, identical)
> Kung said: are classic of heaven,

They bind through the earth
                          and flow
With recurrence,
                 action, humanitas, equity

Canto 106, which deals with the world of the spirit is one of the most sustained lyrical achievements in the poem; of the subject matter, let it suffice to quote again from *Impact*: "Tradition inheres in the images of the gods and gets lost in dogmatic definition". Mr. Pound has made us see again a beauty that has always been there; that the world has forgotten it does not make it any less real:

       not in memory,
             in eternity
                      and 'as a wind's breath
       that changing its direction changeth its name',
                                               Apeliota
       for the gold light of wheat surging upward
                               ungathered
       Persephone in the cotton-field
                 granite next sea wave
       is for clarity
                 deep waters reflecting all fire
       nueva lumbre,
                 Earth, Air, Sea
                      in the flame's barge
       over Amazon, Orinoco, great rivers.

The last three Cantos of *Thrones* are centered around English history and, in particular, the Institutes of Sir Edward Coke

       hospitality. . . of the ancient ornaments and
           commandations of England   (Canto 107)

W. M. Merchant deals with Pound's interest in Coke at greater length than is possible here in an excellent article in the *Yale Literary Magazine* (December 1958) where he quotes a letter from Pound saying, "that I get to Coke via the Sacred Edict, a measure of decay in brit/ and yank/ education." The conception of law as a safeguard against tyrrany adds an essential element that is missing from the Chinese principles of good government expressed in Canto 99, while Coke, in his commentary and collection of the centuries of English law preceding him, is in some ways a Confucian figure. It is fitting, also, that he should come into the poem at this point because he was an important part of Adams' heritage — he first appears in the Adams Cantos. In his fight against King James he is a genuinely heroic figure (his function in Cantos 107–109 is perhaps best defined by a phrase from *Rock-Drill*: "thrones, and above them: Justice") and he is central to the definition of law in the Cantos: "law's aim is against coercion either by force or by fraud". Incidentally the often repeated references to Queen Elizabeth here: "For every new cottage 4 acre Stat. de 31 Eliz./Angliae amor." add another dimension to the mythological treatment she receives in Rock-Drill: "in the Queen's eye the reflection / & seawrack —". *The Cantos* are full of interrelations of the kind noted in this paragraph which is one of the reasons that the world of the poem is such an intensely poetic and coherent one.

Behind all the rage and fragmentation of much of *Thrones* there is often a point of stillness and peace (perhaps connected with Pound's theory of the "great bass") underlying the surface activity of the verse; the sense of a permanent world beyond the merely temporal facts of all the emperors and kings:

> stone to stone, as a river descending
> the sound a gemmed light,
>   form is from the lute's neck.

And, apart from all the history, what makes these cantos succeed are the lines that shine out, from the midst of the sometimes confusing array of historical detail, describing with a precision unequalled by Wordsworth the delicacy and paradisal qualities of nature, whether it is "the coral light sifting slowly mid sea-fans", "The sky . . . leaded with elm boughs" or "Where deer's feet make dust in shadow/ at wood's edge".

In *The Cantos* Pound has resurrected ways of thinking that are still valid, but have been either forgotten or eroded by the deadening forces of modern life. "They make total war on CONTEMPLATIO" (Canto 85)

"Only connect . . ." One measure of the success of the poem is that it has brought things that were previously disjunct without blurring their edges into a permanent pattern of meaning. Another is Pound's capacity for continuous development. *The Cantos* really *is* a record of the growth of a poet's mind.

Perhaps it is one of the tasks of poetry to affirm the existence of paradise even though today it can probably only exist in "the wilds

of a man's mind". Mr Pound in the bits of the poem that have
appeared since *Thrones* is, to quote Keats, "straining for particles
of light in the midst of a great darkness". These cantos make us
realize that he probably over-simplified the world in some earlier
parts of the poem. They are fragments of beauty that because of
their fragmentation are permeated by pain. We publish perhaps the
finest in this issue. It is a cluster of things felt, that spark off new
relationships with themselves and with the body of the work on
each rereading — some more Cantos of this quality should enable
us to see, as in a vision, all parts of the poem draw to a deeper
unity than had once seemed possible. 'Felicem cui datum est dis-
persiones cordis in unum colligere.'

Sister M. Bernetta Quinn, O.S.F.

A Study of *Thrones* by Ezra Pound

Galla Placidia's tomb at Ravenna is composed of tiny bits of
stone, glass, and metals, meaningless in themselves but out of
which artisans have formed a predominantly blue miracle which
immortalizes this sister of the Emperor Honorius and mother of
Valentinian III, a shrine rivaled in Europe only by the color har-
monies of Chartres. *Thrones* serves a similar purpose, the celebration of nobility, in Pound's case as incarnated in a chain of persons
reaching from the time of Homer to the middle of the twentieth
century. He might indeed have been describing his intent when
translating these lines from Horace:

> This monument will outlast metal and I made it
> More durable than the king's seat, higher than the
> pyramids.

Written for this collection. Published by permission of Sister Bernetta Quinn,
O.S.F. Permission to reprint should be obtained from Charles E. Merrill Publishing Company.

Gnaw of the wind and rain?
Impotent
The flow of years to break it, however many.
(*From Confucius to Cummings*, p. 36)[1]

Though "king's seat" is only one connotation of *thrones*, as metaphor it focuses his effort.

Thrones consists of fourteen poems varying in length from three pages to nineteen. Its opening picks up the Greek poem wherewith *Section: Rock-Drill* ends (*Odyssey*, V), re-introducing the beneficient spirit of white-ankled Leucothoe, now a goddess but once a human being, like Pound. Longest in the collection, Canto 96 is also the most difficult to follow. If it is to be more than a "persistent argument," one ought to imagine an interchange of voices, all speaking out of a central consciousness, that of the wanderer who has been moving towards the "crystal sphere" since the Homeric beginnings of Canto 1, written over sixty years ago. The action in the latest book (apart from the 1969 fragments) can be viewed as the rotation of the planet Saturn by those angels known as thrones (*Paradiso*, XXI, l. 25). of which the *lumina mundi* specifically referred to are analogues.

Pound is a universalist. Lamenting the cleavage between East and West, he tries to bring them together, as they were during the Byzantine era. The raft of Odysseus drifts through a Danaan rain of coins, dramatization of a monetary theme which becomes more and more pervasive as the epic continues. Like the fading out of a filmed scene in favor of another, the mythic hero yields to rulers or attackers of the Roman Empire, born in that province of Italy, Tuscany, the name of which, derived from incense, connects it to that sacred used throughout to interrupt fact with its paradisiac visions. In earlier Cantos Pound has extended the glorification of warlords (Sigismundo Malatesta): here, without developing their exploits, he merely indicates Gaulic Brennus and Cunimundus, Lombard Authar, Parthian Chosroes, Roman Tiberius, Ostragoth Theoderic, Longobard Rothar, and others whose deeds are chronicled in Latin by Paul the Deacon, in the Migne edition he was kept supplied with by his Franciscan-friar visitors during the long years at Saint Elizabeth's. Canto 96 emphasizes the contemporaneity of these fragments out of the past by its diction: "dope already used" in the seventh century A.D., corresponding to a sym-

---

[1]Edited with Marcella Spann (New York: New Directions, 1964).

bolic letter of analytic geometry, cannot escape involving its modern counterpart: "The statements of 'analytics' are 'lords' over facts. They are the thrones and dominations that rule over form and recurrence." (*Gaudier-Brzeska*, p. 106).[2]

Places are always important in *The Cantos*, unique and yet interchangeable as are variously carved Kings and Queens in chess. More significant than Bergamo, Brescia, Ticino in Canto 96 is Verona, whose San Zeno was once a magnet to the American expatriate during that season when wanderlust drove him from one sanctuary of Beauty to another:

> The Twelfth Century, or, more exactly, that century whose center is the year 1200, has left us two perfect gifts: the church of San Zeno in Verona, and the canzoni of Arnaut Daniel; by which I would implicate all that is most excellent in the Italian-Romanesque architecture and in Provençal minstrelsy. (*The Spirit of Romance*, p. 22).[3]

The reader is tacitly invited to be *comes itineris* (journey's companion) as Pound proceeds down the path of Roman imperialism, into the reigns of Charlemagne and Peppin. Like the radiant bikini which saves Odysseus from the waves, a light-ideogram appears as *continuum*, for once not taken from the familiar source R. H. Mathews's *A Chinese-English Dictionary*.[4] A Chinese middle name, it is accompanied by a Latin translation meaning "brilliant in act and word," the three languages reminding us that we live on a globe, not just in a hemisphere, continent, country, city.

Conspicuous among the thrones of this involved Canto is Diocletian (d. 313 A.D.), here praised for his complete reform of coinage while conducting the Asiatic affairs of the Empire. Though a neat sequence of dates would be convenient to understanding, such methodology would be uncharacteristic of *The Cantos*, which skip around chronologically among the thrones of Christian Rome: Tiberius of the second century A.D.; Heraclius triumphantly bearing the Holy Cross into Jerusalem five centuries later; Leo VI the Wise; the ill-fated Justinian, unable to hold off the barbarians. For those who want a straight account of Rome's decline and fall in the East, one might recommend J. M. Hussey's *The Byzantine World*,[5] which

---

[2] (London: John Lane, 1916).

[3] (Norfolk, Conn.: New Directions, n.d.)

[4] (Shanghai: China Inland Mission and Presbyterian Mission Press, 1931.)

[5] (New York: Harper & Brothers, 1961.)

narrates how the Bulgars threatened Roman power in the tenth
century. It is hard to make a consecutive pattern out of Pound's
random comments, yet looking backwards over the story of the tribe
of Aeneas after his flight from Troy one intuits, though with
difficulty, a sort of unity:

> Pound's just men are all lawmakers in their way. His important
> political heroes are chosen from periods of history which the poet
> regards as crucial, periods in which there is a renewal of the har-
> mony between man, man's cities, and the process exhibited by the
> particular hero. (Paul A. Olson, "Pound and the Poetry of Per-
> ception," *Thought*, XXXV [Autumn, 1960], p. 340)[6]

Yeats once wished for a reincarnation which would have placed
him back in the finest years of Byzantium. Pound also admired the
financial, political, and social regime of that chapter of civilization.
Relying upon E. H. Freshfield's version of *The Book of the Pre-
fects*, he weaves a composite image around the city, bringing it up
to date with a memory of Yale professor Norman Holmes Pearson
climbing as a tourist all over Santa Sophia in a century when this
building is only something to marvel at out of a dead culture. The
Byzantine cathedral was constructed by that Justinian whom
Dante considered most representative of Roman glory, one of the
thrones of the crowning division of the *Divine Comedy*. Pound's
enthusiasm for this ruler dated from (at least) his own period of
greatest vigor: "But Antoninus, Constantine and Justinian were
serious characters, they were trying to work out an orderly system,
a modus vivendi for vast multitudes of mankind. (*Guide to Kulchur*, p. 40).[7] Canto 96 ends with the single word, in the most fitting
tongue, that summarizes what Justinian strove for: *pacem.*

No short essay could possibly undertake a detailed *explication de
texte* of that portion of Pound's *chef d'oeuvre* still lacking the annotations to which the first books have been subjected. Within a
brief space one can at best merely describe directions, in the present instance as they touch upon the major symbol *thrones*. Related
to both this and a larger unifying motif is the brush stroke on page
8, Chen[4], which also appears on the back cover of the Milan edition
and in Cantos 86 and 91. Mathews defines it as a verb meaning "to
shake, terrify" (p. 39). How quickly the Goddess Fortuna, as Cavalcanti has sung, can topple from their thrones all who are mighty

---

[6]Pp. 331–349.
[7](Norfolk, Conn.: New Directions, n.d.)

under the moon! Very few are asked to experience so bitterly as Pound, in their personal lives, the truth of this fall of princes.

Stepping into the middle of the Odyssean drama, the reader is bound to find Canto 96 stiff going, devoid as it is of lovely imagery and haunting music. Almost none of it is lyrical. The Leucothoe introduction referred to above is an exception, also the poignant couplet "Who shall know throstle's note from banded thrush/ by the wind in the holly bush," apparently impersonal until one adverts to Saint Elizabeth's. Another flash of unmistakable poetry is "Goodbye to the sun, Autumn is dying," followed by "O beautiful Sun" in Greek (p. 15), which likewise has an autobiographical sense in that Wyncote's first name for the boy Ezra was always Ray — the sun-god of Egypt, creator and protector of men, vanquisher of evil.

Canto 97, in the main a history of money, is similar to its predecessor in an absence of song and Botticellian delicacy. When these do appear they tend to be buried in complexity. On page 27 Pound combines English, Latin, Chinese, Greek in his attempt to illustrate the Ling^2 sensibility (cf. the start of *Section: Rock-Drill*) by delineating a unique sunrise color, not flame nor carmine nor brass but russet-gold, a hue inspiring thoughts of Kuanon, goddess of love and mercy (identified with the solace of friendship) and of Berenice, whose hair, consecrated to Venus, was made into stars by Jupiter. If Eliot knew too much when he wrote *The Waste Land* what shall be said of Pound in *Thrones*? And yet his poem is his portrait, and the erudition is part of the man. Moreover, one cannot legislate about subjects. *Polite Essays* makes this clear:

> It makes no difference whether we are writing of money or landscapes. Madox Ford's aim toward the just word was right in his personal circle of reference. He was dealing mainly with visual and oral perceptions, whereinto come only colors, concrete forms, tones of voice, modes of gesure. (p. 53)[8]

In his youth, while visiting the work-site of his father, Pound had absorbed these four types of perception as he watched the newly struck silver, British sovereigns melted and stamped with eagles, shoveled by gas-flares in the depths of the Philadelphia mint. One of the best lines in his entire poem owes something to this recollection: "In the gloom the gold gathers the light about it."

---

[8](Norfolk, Conn.: New Directions, n.d.)

With the Mohammedan conquest of Asia came silver coin put into the hands of the people but also gold pieces minus the Roman Emperor's effigy, a departure from policy which shattered the peace of the land. After alluding to Islam, Pound, with the rapidity of television, turns the attention of Canto 97 to ancient Britain, from whose soil his own ancestors emigrated. After a sampling of personages (Lear, Athelstan, Offa, Henry III), he closes in on the figure whose virtues best demonstrate the idea behind the book's title: Mons of Jute, who "should have his name in the record,/thrones, courage" (p. 24). A chief judge who, unarmed, confronted the tyrannical king of the Danes and forced him to flee, Mons deserves to rank among those of whom Pound said to Donald Hall in a *Paris Review* interview: "The thrones in the *Cantos* are an attempt to move out from egoism and to establish some definitions of an order possible or at any rate conceivable on earth" (*Writers at Work*, II, p. 58).[9] In language, the equivalent of thrones is the combination *chêng*[4] *ming*[2] (p. 34), exact terminology, repeatedly worked into the context of the epic.

Pound customarily shapes his Cantos into blocs: after the first two in *Thrones*, he concentrates on Chinese material. Here his source is the Sacred Edict as translated by a Presbyterian minister F. W. Baller,[10] itself a translation by Salt Works Commissioner Wang-iu-p'uh of an earlier text known as the Sixteen Maxims. Before getting down to his colloquial restatements of Baller's Wang, Pound creates a bright blur of theophany out of references to Egyptian and Greek myth (Ra-Set's sun-boat, Leucothoe transformed to an incense bush in resistance to Apollo); to the holy cities of Leo Frobenius in Africa; to Neo-Platonic light-theories. Sensitive men throughout history have been aware of these theophanies as they occurred, have seen that the snow's lace was like sea-foam. Modern Italy still honors these eternal moments: black shawls for Demeter, the mother of fair Persephone.

Most writers have kept journals: Pound, so far as is known, has not. Yet regarded from one perspective *The Cantos* are his supreme journal of the persons, places, events, books which have been important to him and which such biographical critics as Patricia Hutchins and Charles Norman have sought to arrange. Canto 98 scatters amidst Oriental precepts of conduct memories of Pound's yesteryear friends Yeats, Eliot, Ford, Lewis; of his days as art and

---

[9] (New York: The Viking Press, 1963), pp. 35–61.

[10] (Shanghai: American Presbyterian Mission Press, Second Edition, 1907.)

music critic of London's *The New Age*, under the editorship of Orage; of Noel Stock, who lessened the sameness of his Washington, D.C., confinement; of his taste for Provençal song dating back to Bill Shephard's Hamilton class and here represented by Cuillo d'Alcamo's "Fresca rosa aulentissima"; of his love for Dolmetsch's clavichord, still cherished in the castle at Brunnenburg. Whoever reads *Thrones* will probably have read some if not all of the first ninety-five Cantos and thus will recognize the cumulative effect of these and like references, employed again and again, giving as they were meant to do the sense of a man's interior life going on, a sense of *le moi* constant under shifting circumstances.

Scholars will eventually do for Pound's use of the Sheng Edict what J. M. Sullivan has done for his adaptations of Propertius. Whether their labors will help the great majority of readers better to understand and enjoy *Thrones* is doubtful. On this score one example can stand as "the figure in the carpet," selected for its association with thrones as regal seats, "More solid than pearls or than cassia" (p. 41). The Edict, via Baller, asks of the Buddhists:

> As to His Celestial Excellency the Gemmy Emperor — if indeed there be such a spirit — he is taking it easy in paradise; do you suppose he needs you to model him a gilded image, and build him a house to live in? (p. 79)

This Pound telescopes into what would be a bit of cynicism, were it not softened with humor: "Sitting in heaven he needs you to build him a roof?" Then, a few lines below, he returns to the excerpt, widening his concept of deity: "Does god need a clay model? gilded?" (p. 40).

Canto choices out of the Sheng Edict, however, are usually ethical, not liturgical, as one might expect of a Confucianist. Pound gives practical examples of the five human relations: emperor and minister, father and son, husband and wife, elder and young brother, friend and friend, all of which stem from the upright heart and its behavior, Chinese characters for which began appearing midway through the work, multiplying themselves at this point. All the five relations are condensed in Canto 99's succinct "state, family and friendship" (p. 53). Few areas of behavior escape an injection of Sheng wisdom as Pound cubistically breaks apart and re-combines the Maxims. Though these Cantos parallel the *Divine Comedy* in their preoccupation with morality, Pound is here "the teacher of the mob" rather than a shaper of stories. The Florentine too could wrap himself in the robe of *magister*, though his genius for simile kept fresh the laurel wreath around his temples. Pound's way of retaining, between lessons, what everyone recognizes as poetry is to intersperse flashes of cadenced sense appeal. Canto 99 contains seventeen such lines, beginning with the first two: "Till the blue grass turn yellow/ and the yellow leaves float in air" (p. 46) right down to that hokku "Small birds sing in chorus,/ Harmony is in the proportion of branches." (p. 60)

In youth, Pound, as he writes John Quinn, expected to end his poem with the hundredth Canto (New York Public Library, Manuscript Division, April 11, 1917). Like Whitman, Williams, and Stevens, he came to see that his work, if organic, had to be coterminous with his life. Completed while its author was still in Saint Elizabeth's, on New Year's Day, 1958, Canto 100 has nothing final about it: most of the others in the sequence are far more memorable. Though for over a dozen years Pound has been in what amounted to a prison, untried, like Jo Skelton and Danton, as Odysseus he is still traveling "per plura diafana." Dante by the hundredth Canto had reached the heart of Heaven: Pound remains in Hell, though his agony is here only an echo from the Pisan litany:

> Out of Erebus.
> Where no mind moves at all
> In crystal funnel of air
> Out of heaviness (p. 68)

In his well-known copy of J. Lempriére's *Classical Dictionary*,[11] Pound must have read how the god Erebus, derived from Chaos and Darkness, married Night, by whom he begot the light and the day (p. 301). In the ten pages of this Canto, light furnishes some exquisite effects. Inspired as so often by Dante, the poet rises to an apex of synaesthesia: "stone to stone, as a river descending/ the sound a gemmed light" (p. 68). If Odysseus is a man on whom the sun has gone down, like Erebus he may yet give birth to light: "a green yellow flash after sunset" and again, the translation of the ideogram *pai jih*, "in the white light." Scraps of the Sheng Edict come back, like the repetitions of conversation, with punctuation to note that Pound is aware he is quoting his own earlier Cantos. Two instances on p. 71 of the Ming[2] ideogram, sun and moon joined, remind us of Chinese and scholastic light-metaphysics and urge the

---

[11]*Bibliotheca Classica* or *Classical Dictionary* (London: John Bone, 1828).

poet onwards: despite all the "unthrones" that trouble his imagination, he has a sure promise that the gods have willed his return to Ithaca.

Suddenly the Cantos become very brief (101, 102). They are like speeches of a mountain-climber in pauses during an ascent. The environs are those of China, as experienced vicariously through the pages of anthropologist Joseph Rock,[12] wherein a primitive tribe dignifies life by ceremonies centering around the juniper tree, in a communal regard felt only by individuals in a more sophisticated society. "*Thrones* concerns the states of mind of people responsible for more than their personal conduct," Pound told Donald Hall, the *Paris Review* interviewer (*Writers at Work*, II, p. 58). Canto 101 commends a number of such men: Charles Talleyrand (1754–1838) and Louis Thiers (1797–1877), French statesmen who "tried to get sense into princes"; the Roman economist Del Pelo Pardi, a family friend of the Pounds who later was to go to Cuba to aid its agricultural reforms; Plotinus; other characters from history whose identities are perhaps no more requisite for appreciation than the originals of "Mauberley."

Canto 102 recapitulates the Odyssean theme, bringing back in the thoughts of the hero the pledge of his safe return to Ithaca, sent him from Zeus through Hermes and Calypso. Landscape images of an eternal world make tolerable the present: the incense bush, disguise of Leucothoe; a snow lacy as foam; the silver rocks of cloud-covered Li-Chiang with its wild geese, pine trees ablaze, salt and veins of copper; russet-gold sunlight (oriXalko), carrying the poem back to Venus with whom the Greek word was associated in Canto I.

Human beings cannot bear very much reality: Canto 103 has no trace of an enduring Eden. Tags snipped out of Pound's reading as mentioned earlier suggest how uneasy lies our globe under the hand of Fortuna. Thrones here range from Thaddeus Coleman Pound, the author's grandfather who played an honorable part in Wisconsin public affairs of the nineteenth century, to the Iron Chancellor Otto Bismarck (1815–1898), who in founding the German Empire aimed at a permanent peace after 1870. Rock's [1]Na-[2]Khi villagers of northern China reappear as Canto 104 opens, as does the ideogram for Ling[2] sensibility, three mouths ("voices") under a cloud, heavily marked in Pound's copy of Mathews ("the spirit of a being which acts upon others," p. 586): pondering this definition, one

---

[12]"The [2]Muàn [1]Bpö Ceremony or the Sacrifice to Heaven as Practiced by the [1]Na-[2]khi," *Monumentica Serica*, XIII (1948), 1–160.

can readily see the reason why the Chinese character stands as decoration for the front cover of Vanni Scheiwiller's Italian edition of *Thrones*.[13] Also braided into the title-symbolism is a term near the conclusion of Canto 104: Monreale, splendid church at Palermo, the name of which joins the words of Dante's phrase *lo real manto* (*Paradiso*, XXIII, l. 113), of which Pound wrote in the first version of his *The Spirit of Romance*: "With what Homeric majesty and what simplicity falls his epithet for that sphere which whirls the largest, the *primum mobile*, most violent of the concentric spheres" (p. 157). Then comes the third strand of throne-connotation, echoed from Canto 88, a seat wrought of solid light for divine majesty: "Topaz, God can sit on."

The principal throne in Canto 105 is Saint Anselm. Pound once remarked that he would become a Catholic if he could pick his own theologians, one of whom would unquestionably be this great ecclesiastic following Lanfranc as Archbishop of Canterbury. First to try to derive the idea of God from human reason, Anselm with his *rationalem* was possibly the source of the *intenzione* of Guido Cavalcanti, whom Pound feels certain also read the *Monologion*. Like the author of the *Cantos*, he was forced into exile, his crime being the refusal to pay a promotion-tax required by Rufus, son of William the Conqueror. This Canto is thickly populated with other early Englishmen: the Mercian king Ethelbald; Athelstan; Egbert; Ethelfled; the incorruptible Canute.

How pleasing is the return from chronicle to lyricism in Cantos 106 and 107. Although little in the images is new they here combine into an oasis; another way of putting it is that they are song, punctuated by spaces of talk. Persephone, to Pound a private as well as a cultural symbol, is the central feminine figure, as different from Circe as glen from sea, the juniper her sacred bush. "In *Thrones* Persephone's tragedy is over: she has returned; her trees are in blossom," says Guy Davenport in Eva Hesse's *New Approaches to Pound* (p. 159).[14] Other women here testify that absolute beauty exists: Helen, Athena, Artemis, Selena, Aphrodite. Diverse lights fuse into a subdued glow, prelude to the "crystal sphere" towards which the whole poem mounts.

Deprived of his only daughter's presence as she opens like a rose, Pound begins Canto 107 with the azalea, "grown while we sleep" (p. 108). Illustrious throne in this Canto is "the clearest mind ever

[13] (Milan: All 'Insegna del Pesce d'Oro, 1956).

[14] (Berkeley and Los Angeles: University of California Press, 1969), pp. 145–74, "Persephone's Ezra."

in England," Sir Edward Coke, Chief Justice under James II and famous for the four-part *Institutes* admired by Pound for its precision and thirst for justice. Joining that brotherhood in the Cantos who stand up for their beliefs against authority, Coke had his career crushed by the force he opposed (in 1616 he was the only judge out of twelve to resist James). Pound links him as hero with Kung; the Pythagorean philosopher Ocellus; scientist Louis Agassiz; and that friend of his Kensington days Gaudier-Brzeska.

England, rather than late-medieval Italy, China in its highest dynasties, and young America, furnishes the thrones in Cantos 108 and 109, not the least being that Edward who relinquished his sceptre through love of a woman, before he had a chance to act the part of good governor. From Pound's childhood home in Wyncote, or perhaps from his mother's library when she died in Rapallo, the poet kept John Richard Green's *History of the English People*,[15] a two-volume work inscribed "Mrs. Weston, Xmas, 1882" (his grandmother) and very much marked up by him, as he pursued through reading what Canto 108 calls in its final two words "Angliae amor," a labor undertaken, as its opening states, "Pro Veritate" (in behalf of truth). One is tempted to agree with Poe's "The Poetic Principle" that truth is inimical to beauty: yet the individual lines wait, like the pieces at Ravenna, to be subsumed into that design which is the "lifetime" of the *Cantos*, an art to be studied neither too close up nor too far away.

Before ending *Thrones*, Pound once again pays homage to Beauty deified:

> Clear deep off Taormina
> high cliff and azure beneath it
> form is cut in the lute's neck, tone is from the bowl
> Oak boughs alone over Selloi
> This wing, colour of feldspar

Like the blue jay that Cummings compared him to, he flashes off "Over wicket gate," but not before leaving in our minds that abrupt directive from Dante: "You in the dinghey (piccioletta) astern there!" (*Paradiso*, II, l. 1) No throne in the epic is brighter than Dante; he who in *Paradiso*, IX, calls this angelic hierarchy Cunizza's mirrors, reflecting the mind of God (ll. 61–62).

---

[15] (New York: Wm. L. Allison & Son, 1882.)

Considered in its entirety, *Thrones* might best be described as reflections. *The Cantos* will never merge into a single artifact as intelligible as Galla Placidia's tomb, but then they are not a tomb. They are intimations of immortality, together with records of the best and worst in mortality. If their whole is to equal the sum of its parts — that is, if the Cantos are to become *The Cantos* — *Thrones* like the earlier books needs to be recognized as essential to the total effect of Pound's "speech for contemplation." The Pilgrim Poet invites; let who will accept.